"Through the authentic, captivating, com··· *I Am Rahab*, Autumn Miles presents a be··· grace of God and the hope he gives. Grounded ··· book is a great encouragement to all who believe they are beyon··· God's reach and restoration. Autumn explores the life of Rahab and moves readers to look beyond themselves and see the forgiveness and mission God has for their lives. A thought-provoking and inspiring read for anyone seeking hope."

Monica Rose Brennan
Associate professor & director of women's ministries
at Liberty University

"You *must* read this book! As Autumn Miles bares her soul and secrets, she also creatively and powerfully uses the story of Rahab to show the redemption, restoration, and adoration the Lord has for his sweet beloved. *I Am Rahab* is truly for those who think that their sins are too great to be cleansed, their mistakes are too awful to be forgiven, and their brokenness is too immense to be healed. Any victim—in or out of the horrors of sex trafficking or *any* kind of abuse—will be able to relate to the timely words in this book. Through these pages they, too, will soon realize that the fierce and redemptive love of God for the broken is bigger than any hurt, pain, or mistake they've made, and that God can use any circumstance for his good!"

Annie Lobert
President and founder of Hookers for Jesus

"Autumn Miles has a heart for the Lord and for people. One thing I love about her is that she is good at saying the things that need to be said for the good of her brothers and sisters in Christ and for the glory of God. She has a story and a message that exude hope and the faithfulness of the Lord."

Mary Kate Robertson
TheLittleDuckwife.com

"*I Am Rahab* is one of the most in-depth looks at the beautiful story of redemption through the eyes of one of the most unlikely—Rahab. This powerful book reminds us that God's grace is unchanging, unwavering, and unflinching. Autumn Miles takes us on a remarkable journey, making it clear to each of us that the cross does have the final word."

Oneka McClellan
Lead pastor of Shoreline City

"*I am* is a powerful, empowering declaration. *I am* is the name God chooses to reveal his character, and as God's image bearers it is the essence of who we are. Through sin and pain and abuse, the Enemy seeks to steal and kill and destroy our sense of the *I am*—and the *I am* sense of ourselves. Autumn Miles shares her journey back to *I am* and invites the reader to do the same by listening, searching God's Word, and responding in obedience. *I Am Rahab* reveals the path toward redemption and joy, which God offers to us all. For those in darkness, this is light. For those in pain, this is balm."

Carmen LaBerge
Radio host, author, speaker at ReconnectWithCarmen.com

"What is your Jericho? What is holding you back? Do you feel that your past determines your future? This book digs into the life of Rahab and unwraps how God will unlock your past to promote your future. Autumn Miles writes with extraordinary transparency about her sinful past, and with timeless wisdom she shares how God used every hurt in her life as an opportunity. Autumn is a master storyteller and clearly a voice to this generation! *I Am Rahab* will demand a second reading to get out all that God has put in!"

Lisa Kratz Thomas
Author of *This Is Your Life—Not a Dress Rehearsal*
and *Light in Our Darkness*

I AM RAHAB

Touched by God, Fully Restored

Autumn Miles

WORTHY®
PUBLISHING

Published by Worthy Books, an imprint of Worthy Publishing Group, a division of Worthy Media, Inc., One Franklin Park, 6100 Tower Circle, Suite 210, Franklin, TN 37067.

WORTHY is a registered trademark of Worthy Media, Inc.
HELPING PEOPLE EXPERIENCE THE HEART OF GOD

eBook available wherever digital books are sold.

Library of Congress Cataloging-in-Publication Data

Names: Miles, Autumn, author.
Title: I am Rahab : touched by God, fully restored / Autumn Miles.
Description: Franklin, TN : Worthy Publishing, 2018. | Includes
  bibliographical references.
Identifiers: LCCN 2018022248 | ISBN 9781683972693 (tradepaper)
Subjects: LCSH: Rahab (Biblical figure)
Classification: LCC BS580.R3 M55 2018 | DDC 222/.2092--dc23
LC record available at https://lccn.loc.gov/2018022248

For foreign and subsidiary rights, contact rights@worthypublishing.com

The author is represented by Ambassador Literary Agency, Nashville, TN.

ISBN: 978-1-68397-269-3

Cover design by Marc Whitaker, MTW Designs
Interior design by Bart Dawson

Printed in the United States of America
18 19 20 21 22 LSC 8 7 6 5 4 3 2 1

———•••———

Thanks to my most precious Jesus,
who is the reason I live, breathe, and have hope.

And to my husband and children,
who have taught me how to truly live. I adore you.

———•••———

CONTENTS

A Prayer for My Readers   vii

1. I AM RAHAB   1

2. I AM AUTUMN   13

3. I AM NOT ONE SEASON   27

4. I AM LISTENING   43

5. I AM RISK   57

6. I AM FLAWED   71

7. I AM SACRIFICE   85

8. I AM GOD'S INSIDE MAN   99

9. I AM A CHANGED WORLD   111

10. I AM ON TIME   129

11. I AM INTEGRITY   145

12. I AM A CONQUEROR   159

13. I AM NEW   171

Discussion Questions   183

Notes   211

A PRAYER FOR MY READERS

Lord, God Almighty, I pray that all who read the pages of this book are challenged to possess the fullness of what you have set apart for them. I pray Rahab's story encourages them and shifts their hearts. I pray, oh good God, that your grace would encourage them like never before. I pray, awesome God, that you will give them the strength and boldness to step out in great faith and to do the things you've asked of them as doers of the Word. I pray, God, that they remember they are not alone, and that you have called them to new. I pray, Lord Jesus, that you would surround them with your wisdom and protection. Lord, change lives through the pages of this book and the profound Word of the Lord.

In Jesus's name, amen

Chapter One

———•••———

I AM RAHAB

If I turn up dead, look at him first," I said in a shaky whisper. I sat completely still, glaring emotionless down at the mint chocolate chip ice cream I attempted to enjoy, not knowing how my sister would take the sentence.

She froze, her spoon halfway to her mouth. I finished my breath. The carbon dioxide released in my exhalation felt small in comparison to the weight of stress obliterated when I uttered those words. I'd been carrying suffocating stress for nearly six years. Finally, the secret was out. I had finally gathered the courage and voiced my greatest fear.

For several seconds, my older sister, Heather, scrambled for the right words to counter such a horrifying declaration. "What?" she asked.

I couldn't look at her. The strategic positioning of the chocolate chips in my ice cream entranced me. I kept my attention on them long enough to breathe out the heavy words once more. I repeated them louder and clearer this time, "If I turn up dead, look at him first." The words fell easier from my mouth. I looked around to see if anyone else had heard me.

Although my heart was still beating and I was breathing, I felt that my soul had died. My outward appearance reflected my inner state of mind. I had shut off my emotions a year earlier when the daily abuse I encountered hurt so much both emotionally and physically. Honestly, the pain felt so acute, I didn't care if he did kill me. Maybe I even wanted it. God knows I thought of killing myself. I envisioned it many times because I imagined the end would at least bring finality to my suffering.

I had lived the last six years in an abusive relationship, from dating to marriage. My circumstances had been, in part, a repercussion of my own choices. Before I was married, I had done everything I could to rebel against God. My lifestyle had been one of sin. Lying, sexual immorality, and manipulation had all been normal behaviors for me. I had allowed myself to be subjected to a man whose first and primary attraction to me was purely lust. When the lust had been satisfied, his desire turned to control. My sin had propelled me into a living hell I helped create.

My once bubbly, vivacious personality had changed dramatically under the control of a man who dominated me day in and day out. I had become a robot. I was behaving mindlessly, brainwashed by the harsh orders and crippling fear of a man whom I claimed to love. I was his puppet, forbidden to wear certain clothing without his permission and censored in my speech. I might as well have been in a cult. I was a silent walking billboard for abuse.

But on a spring day in Indiana, the pressure of my silence, held for so many years as a false sense of protection, erupted like a volcano. And for the first time ever, I gave my silence a voice and shared my concern about my then husband.

My sister sat there, shocked. She was quiet for a moment and then replied again, "What? What are you talking about?" My two previous announcements gave me courage, something I had lacked for almost six years. It shattered the dirt-smothered ceiling of my emotional grave, and I finally began to tell my sister of the horror I was living in. Even though the threat of my own death fell out of my mouth, its admission seemed to somehow give me life.

By the time I finished speaking, the scoops of ice cream had turned to spoonfuls of soup. The despair in my heart, though, had also begun to melt away at the surrender of my oppressive secret. I knew my sister wasn't the answer to my abusive marriage, but I tasted hope in sharing with her; something about it fueled the idea of freedom. I'd been emotionally deceased, physically violated, socially cast out, and spiritually dry. My uninhibited outpour awoke something in me, and I wanted more.

One night, shortly after that ice cream date with my sister, I could not sleep. I was convinced that my husband was going to kill me. As I lay in bed plotting to kill myself, I realized how scared of death I was and that I could no longer take my life. During those moments in the dark, I heard the Spirit of the living God whisper to me, "Do you remember me?" I sat up at full attention, knowing God was speaking. With my father as a pastor, I had been raised in the church and had heard about God my whole life. I had committed my life to him, but that night I heard his voice in a new way. It wasn't harsh. It wasn't angry with me, as I believed God was. The voice was loving. Somehow this one, gentle, probing question brought me hope. It was so soft but authoritative. It knew me; it knew where I was. The power of his whisper drew me out of bed.

I walked to the other room and in anger fought the righteousness pursuing me. I didn't want it. I was mad at it, but I needed it. I felt it had left me when I needed it most. Yet in the height of the consequences of deliberate sin, God intervened. He met me there. Right there. The anger gave way to surrender as the voice of Almighty God continued to penetrate my emotionally sick soul. I cried out, "God, I don't believe in you! I haven't seen any miracles. I've heard the stories, but where is this God of the Bible? Even though I don't believe, if you are the God you say you are, you better speak now." All I knew was that if God didn't end this, I would.

I then opened up an old Bible, and my eyes rested on this promise to those who put their faith in God: "With a long life I will satisfy him and let him see My salvation" (Psalm 91:16). When my eyes met that line, I crumbled in surrender on the floor. There was no church hipster worship leader singing the latest praise song and no majestic light show programmed with a fog machine to set a certain atmosphere. There was no tattooed preacher sharing about Jesus and no one to impress. It was just me before the Lord, raw and sinful and at the end of myself. And right there, I found Jesus. I met my Creator. Sin had gotten me there, but grace would carry me forward.

A MESS LIKE ME

With this newfound depth of revelation with God, I started searching Scripture for someone to whom I could relate. My hunger for the Word of God was insatiable. I was consumed, and many characters caught my attention. I reread about Mary, the mother of Jesus, wondering if I could relate to her. The Bible says she was "highly favored" (Luke 1:28 NIV), and I stopped there. I didn't feel highly favored. I felt more like a total screwup. Don't get me wrong. I gave Mary crazy respect, but this girl couldn't relate.

I kept reading, trying to find comfort in the context of familiarity. I then looked to Esther. She was a Jew living in exile in the land of her enemies, but in a way only God could orchestrate, she became queen of the Persian Empire. Because of her role as queen and accessibility to the king, she was able to later make an appeal on behalf of her people. She saved the Jews from a pending genocide issued by the king. Though her story was amazing, I wasn't there quite yet.

Mary and Esther were examples of what I desperately wanted to become, but I wasn't even on the same hemisphere. Instead, these ladies represented the way I held other women in my mind. The ones acing their Bible drills in Sunday school. The ones saving themselves for marriage and wearing purity rings. As much as I wished, I just wasn't like them.

For a time, Eve felt relatable. Her sin caused the downfall of the human race. Yes, such devastation and wreckage was more familiar. The Lord knows I was experiencing the severe backlash of my own sin. Familiarity struck me again when I later found Jezebel. She was steeped in the depths of sin with her idol worship. I worshipped my husband as a god. He, not the true God, had become my everything. I worshipped his every move and bowed to his human altar. Jezebel was consumed by her evil desires and did not turn to the Lord. She used her influence for destruction and died a gruesome death as Israel's most wicked queen. It was a sobering story. I didn't want my own idol worship to destroy my life or the lives of those I loved.

The utter fallen humanity of Eve and Jezebel felt relatable. And the gravity of their decisions could not be ignored. But I knew there was more—there must be. I was determined to become something greater than my current self, like a Mary or Esther, even though my beginning looked a bit more like Eve or Jezebel. I wanted to shatter the bonds of my past and of other people's expectations. I was desperate to be someone new, to do things new, and to point others to this unshakeable hope I knew was mine.

In spite of my circumstances and past sin, I began to believe that I could be different. Because of God's grace and mercy, I could participate in God's story and help others change their lives. The idea of it swelled inside me. But where was my poster child of hope in Scripture? Hello! Hadn't others royally screwed up their lives as

I had done but still discovered the hope and promise of a changed life through God's supernatural works?

And then I found my girl! The hero God placed in Scripture to speak to me. The one I could relate to, strive to be like, and from whom I could draw hope. I discovered Rahab, the harlot in the second chapter of Joshua. I couldn't read the story fast enough as I gleaned every piece of strength I could.

Rahab was an Amorite who lived in Jericho, a city God had promised to the Israelites. Her life was immersed in sin and the worship of pagan gods. Even her very name reflected this idolatry. The name *Rahab* gives respect to *Ra*, the chief god of the Egyptians, the sun god.[1] She captured my attention with the very first verse: "Then Joshua son of Nun secretly sent two spies from Shittim. 'Go, look over the land,' he said, 'especially Jericho.' So they went and entered the house of a prostitute named Rahab and stayed there" (Joshua 2:1 NIV).

I read furiously. Rahab came face to face with two men whose lives and faith differed from her own. Their presence pointed to the impending destruction of her city and its people.

Endangering her very own life, she made a choice to hide the spies and protected them even further when Jericho's king questioned her about their whereabouts. The king sought to kill them, but she risked her life to protect them. Once the king's men left the city to pursue the spies, she went back to the spies' hiding place, and I caught a glimpse of her heart in the words she spoke to them.

She knew what was about to go down. And she acknowledged it was the Lord who was giving them the city of Jericho. Stories of the Lord's great acts swirled around her, like the miraculous parting of the Red Sea and the killing of two enemy kings. She knew the threat was serious. She knew the Lord would allow the Israelites to defeat Jericho.

And she went on to make this bold request: "Now then, please swear to me by the LORD that you will show kindness to my family, because I have shown kindness to you" (Joshua 2:12 NIV). The spies passionately agreed.

Later, when the day came for Jericho to be destroyed, the spies kept their promise. Rahab and her family were kept safe and spared from death, while her city was completely destroyed, and every person and animal in it was put to death by the sword.

A daring decision, influenced because of her receptivity, faith, and risk, saved her and changed everything. It changed her life. It changed the life of her immediate family. It changed her job and position. It even changed the lives of the Israelite spies. And it would alter a family lineage to come.

And there it was—the kind of story I wanted for my life.

A life entrenched in the depths of sin didn't remain wrecked. Rahab didn't remain a prostitute living in the city walls of Jericho; she dwelled with the Israelites as one of them. She would go on to marry Salmon, one of the two spies she sheltered, and bear a son named Boaz. According to Matthew 1:5, Jesus would be born from this family line. God placed Jesus in a harlot's bloodline. A pagan-worshipping prostitute was ordained to be part of the royal genealogy of Jesus, the Son of the living God. God himself approved a move no legalist would approve of. Which told me this: there was room for me.

I exhaled deeply over the life-altering chapters of Rahab's story, just as I had done that day staring down at mint green chocolate chip ice cream. Her story didn't end just because she lived a lifestyle of sin. God chose her with greater things in mind long before she was born. Greater than she could have ever known when she hid two spies under drying flax stalks on her roof. Even though she may have thought she was choosing to risk her life for God, God chose her for the risk, knowing what she was capable of. He knew his purposes would prevail, and true risk was nullified.

Because I was able to put myself in her story, hope filled my heart and invigorated me. I saw myself in her. I was Rahab, just in a different time and culture. She was a mess. I was too. I never sold my body for money, but I did manipulate people for position. I didn't live in the pagan city of Jericho, but I did live in the bondage of a marriage devoid of God. Her sin, her living position, her imposed identity, and even the time of year she helped the spies resonated with me. But I got the other side of her too: her risk, her faith, the hope bursting forth at the end of her story, and her placement by God in the bloodline of Jesus. All these things were preaching to me. Hope was kindling the fire of my courage. And the narrative in my head shifted.

God chose Rahab. God also chose me.

THE HEART OF A HARLOT

Harlot to hero. I considered both of the titles. I wonder how the descriptions sit with you. Maybe you relate entirely. Because like me, when you look in the mirror, you don't see Mary or Esther. No, you see Rahab staring back. You may not be a prostitute or in a godless relationship you helped create, but you resonate with the way sin defined so much of her life. Or maybe you don't think you relate to Rahab at all. You've sinned. Sure. But it doesn't feel as bad as the lifestyle Rahab lived.

While studying the Bible, I found Rahab isn't relatable to just me. You may be able to relate more than you think. When Rahab is talked about, you will see "harlot" attached to her name. In the Hebrew language of the Old Testament, the word for harlot is *zanah*, which refers to fornication, including the specific instances of a woman who sells her body for sexual uses.[2] In the Greek language of the New Testament, the term *harlot* is *pornē*.[3] Sounds familiar, doesn't it? It should, since this is the root word from which we get the word *pornography*.

The term used to label Rahab captures more than what you may initially think. Hang with me here while I geek out on you. *Both* the Old and New Testament words for harlot can refer to idolatry. Hello! Idolatry is when something or someone has a greater hold on our lives than God. Or we worship anything other than the one true God. In other words, the term *harlot* expands across the boundaries of physical activity to encompass the heart.

The book of Jeremiah gives us further support. Here, the same term used to describe Rahab is used in relation to the nations of Israel and Judah:

> [T]he LORD said to me, "Have you seen what faithless Israel has done? She has gone up on every high hill and under every spreading tree and has committed adultery there. I thought that after she had done all this she would return to me but she did not, and her unfaithful sister Judah saw it. I gave faithless Israel her certificate of divorce and sent her away because of all her adulteries. Yet I saw that her unfaithful sister Judah had no fear; she went out and committed adultery." (3:6–8 NIV)

In this instance, the word *harlot* refers to the nation's unfaithfulness to God. Same word with multiple meanings. As this blunt passage shows, there's more to Rahab's sinful life than just the literal selling of her body for money. Don't discredit your connection to Rahab too quickly until you consider the comprehensive meaning of harlotry to include idolatry. God's use of the same word to describe Rahab's harlotry or Israel's and Judah's unfaithfulness reflects this truth: they're basically the same thing.

The Bible says that "all have sinned and fall short of the glory of God" (Romans 3:23). You and me. Now it's easier to see how the "harlot" can be us, isn't it? In the context of unfaithfulness or idolatry, the message of Rahab just got a lot more relatable.

The culture we live in is saturated with idolatry. If Satan can get us to worship anything other than the one true God, he can take our life and use it for his destructive purposes. Satan can also discount the glory of God and tempt us to add him to a list of gods we worship. God becomes just another god to many. He sits on the same priority shelf with cars, houses, perfectionism, self, money, followers, dreams, social media, relationships, kids, etc. But he then ceases to be worshipped as he deserves, and we become the harlot without even realizing it. I know this is heavy, but in order to move from *harlot* to *hero*, we must confront idolatry.

But here is what I love about Rahab's story. It doesn't end at harlot. It shifts into a story of hope. And perhaps hope—a jarring encounter—is where you count yourself out of the story. Rahab the harlot feels relatable, but not Rahab the hero. You have a hard time believing your life could be anything different. You want to stop settling for less. You want to believe all the Instagram memes that preach of the promises of God. But you are stopped by your own doubt. You have a hard time comprehending you're good enough to become anything, much less a pivotal figure in God's kingdom. Once Rahab began living with the Israelites and assuming all the blessings of God, did you have a hard time hanging out with her? Just as God's plans for Rahab were different from her own, his plans for you are just as amazing. He did not count her out. *Nor* does he count you out.

THE HEART OF A HERO

Rahab didn't look much like a hero when she was introduced in Joshua. But Rahab proved to be more than her occupation. She displayed great strength of ability because she risked her life for the two spies and creatively hid them on her roof. She showed great vision in asking the Israelites to save her life and her family's in exchange for their protection. She showed rare and bold courage in her willingness to leave behind everything she knew—her city, her home, her way of life, her source of provision—and fully immerse herself in the ways of a people group she did not know. She was legendary.

Maybe you don't feel like much of a hero. Maybe you don't think you have the potential for great courage because all you can see is your sin. Nothing feels legendary about your journey. But here is the truth: It doesn't matter whether your sin is private or public. Whether you are a harlot, a stripper, a gossiper. Whether you worship the idol of perfection. Whether you are cheating on your mate, stealing money, heavy in an addiction, or lying all the time. No, your sin is not more powerful than the sacrifice of Jesus, which paid the penalty for your sin. Period! And he sees you differently. He sees you as righteous according to 2 Corinthians 5:21: "[God] made Him who knew no sin to be sin on our behalf, so that we might become the righteousness of God in Him."

Just as Rahab the harlot became Rahab the hero, God wants you to become who he created you to be in spite of your sin. He doesn't *need* you to accomplish his purposes, but he wants you to. God wants you, exactly where you are, knowing exactly where you have been, to join him in his story. We hear the phrase "I want to be used" often in our Christian culture. It is a foreign language to those outside the walls of the church, but it's validated by those within.

Selfish gain was the epitome of man's fallen ways and it was all Rahab knew from those who had used her for her services. But she didn't want to be used; she wanted to be *chosen*. She wanted the God so famous for his might to save her and her loved ones. She wanted it so badly that she risked everything for it. She simply wanted to be chosen by God and saved.

God didn't want to "use" Rahab for his selfish gain. God instead wanted her to join him in what he had already planned for her. She had no idea she was chosen to be a part of God's story from before the day she was born. She already had a seat at God's table, as a daughter or son would. She just hadn't sat down yet. When the spies showed up at her door, she seized the opportunity to join God in his story.

You, too, have always been a part of God's story, even before you were born. The Bible says, "Before I formed you in the womb I knew you, and before you were born I consecrated you; I have appointed you a prophet to the nations" (Jeremiah 1:5). When God spoke these words to Jeremiah, it was clear Jeremiah was set apart to participate in the greater glorious story. Don't be so simpleminded as to believe you are here for your story only. His divine plan for your life is integrated into his indescribable plans for the nations. You are a vital part, with a mission that was ordained before birth.

As we follow Rahab's journey from drying stalks on a roof, to binding a scarlet rope, to leaving all of her known ways and marrying an honorable man, to even being positioned to leave a legacy resulting in the Christ child, I pray you are enlightened to the great story God has created specifically for you. I pray you see the open invitation to join him in what he wants to do through you. If he chose a harlot like Rahab, he also chose you. Just as the Israelites took in Rahab as their own and her life was redefined by the ways of God, God wants to do the same for you. His way of grace and rescuing love will redefine you. You can become a hero no matter how unlikely it seems to you today.

Chapter Two

I AM AUTUMN

I walked into the attorney's office with my twenty-two-year-old legs trembling. I did not know what to expect. The office alone was enough to intimidate me to leave. I was with my mother, who graciously came with me as I took steps to begin the end of a two-and-a-half-year marriage to my abusive husband. Neither one of us spoke as we sat in the waiting room, ready for my name to be called. The clock ticking caught my attention. It felt abnormally loud, striking against the edges of my nerves. Divorce. Divorce at the age of twenty-two. *Who does that? Am I really doing this?* I kept rhetorically asking myself the same questions.

"Autumn, he will see you now," the receptionist said with a smiled, breaking through my thoughts. I smiled nervously. I knew she could read the anxiety on my face. I stood confidently, though, knowing God was releasing me from my toxic marriage. When I entered the office, kind eyes greeted me. They were not ones I expected from an attorney. Welcoming my mom and me as we took our seats, he opened with a question, "What can I do for you?"

I paused, collected my courage, and then stated, "I want a

divorce, and I have heard you are the best lawyer in town. I would like you to take my case." He smiled and I started to relax. I took a deep breath and then unloaded on him the events of the last three years; he hardly looked up as he penned multiple pages of notes. My two and a half years of hell were falling onto the lines of his yellow notepad. Their linear boundaries were catching what was in chaos. When I finished blurting out every pertinent detail I could think of, he looked at me and said, "Autumn, I have three daughters, and as a father I am sorry for what you have gone through." I could see a picture of his beautiful family on his desk. Something softened in me after his statement. I felt a further sense of release.

He went on and stated his usual rate for a divorce. When I heard the number, I felt a little deflated until he added, "But for you, I'll do this divorce for five hundred dollars." What? Even I, broke, could come up with that! With tears in my eyes, I thanked him. This was a miracle. I walked out of the office knowing God had done the impossible. It was my water-to-wine, feed-the-five-thousand, blind-to-see, deaf-to-hear, Lazarus-come-forth miracle. God did the unthinkable for me.

• • •

At this time of my life, my dad had been pastoring a small Baptist church on the north side of an Indiana town for about twenty years. I knew after I decided to divorce my ex-husband, especially once I'd set things into motion legally, my reputation would precede me. And I would have to deal with it. I was right. At the tender age of twenty-two, I boasted a new shiny title: *divorcée*. "There's Autumn, the pastor's daughter who divorced her husband" was how people began referring to me.

"Autumn the divorcée" rang in my ears. Satan used it as a means to kick me while I was down. As if the pain of divorce in my early twenties wasn't hard enough, the extra credential added to my name was salt to my gaping wound. I knew people were talking about me. The rumors were swirling, and I did my best to circumvent the pang of them. Friends would ask, "Is it true that you got divorced?" I would sometimes play dumb and say, "What are you talking about?" just because I wanted to see their response. Maybe, if I'm honest, a part of me wanted them to recite the gossip to my face they so willingly engaged in behind my back. Other times I would race to bring up the topic first. "Did you hear I am divorced now?" My preemptive posture was steeped in self-protection. Over time I realized my behavior in these conversations was because I assumed the label others assigned me. *Divorcée*. I identified myself by it, and people's stinging words confirmed it.

Ugh! I hated it! I still do. I wanted to get rid of that title but didn't know how. I would catch myself wondering what it would be like to live without the title I helped create. It kept me awake at night. How would it affect my future mate? My dreams of adoption and having kids? And what about my dreams to be in ministry? Would churches even accept me? I knew this label could tank opportunities for me. Oh, how it terrorized me for a time. I had earned it. But even though it was a true description, I realized I didn't have to live under its stigma. Yes, I was a divorced twenty-something, but as I grew in knowing the true God, I learned his grace was greater than this ugly title I hated so much.

I remember driving to a hardware store with my dad during this period, and as most dads of adult daughters tend to do, he lovingly began interrogating me on my plans for the future. How would I provide for myself? Where was I going to live? His questions included all the basic ones we love our protective dads for asking. For the first time, I opened up about my doubts that churches would accept me because of my scarlet letter *D*. I felt God calling me to ministry, though I wasn't sure in what capacity. The judgment of religion weighed heavy on my mind and often as I dreamed of my future.

My dad interrupted, and with a stern but loving tone that only a father can use, he corrected me and said, "Autumn, your divorce doesn't define you. Don't define yourself by it or let anyone define you by it. It is merely something God has brought you through. It is a piece of your past and a point of victory for you." After dropping these truth bombs, he continued driving to the hardware store in service to his honey-do list. His five words of genius exploded in my heart: *your divorce doesn't define you.*

It was a moment for me. It stopped me. It somehow freed me from the grip of that title on my life. I could not continue giving it power. No matter how long it took, I was determined to retrain my mind. I recited to myself, "There is now no condemnation for those who are in Christ Jesus" (Romans 8:1). Satan lost the battle over my thoughts.

Slightly terrified of the backlash in my community but confident in God's grace, I started to share my story. With divorce rates up to 50 percent, I knew my title would help me minister. Soon enough, the title I loathed began to let me identify with those who had a similar past or whose lives were messes because of something else. People who never opened up to me before began opening up, thanking me for sharing and being honest about my life. The transparency preached. The honesty was brutal, but it brought hope to those who heard it. The wall of perfectionism I was once proud of suddenly fell like the walls of Jericho. I had once felt safe and strong within that solid barrier, but I had been deceived for way too long. I was surprised to discover that greater strength came when I let others into my imperfect soul. For the first time in my life, I gloried in my weakness, which had become a weapon against evil. My divorce would no longer be used for Satan's purpose; from then on, the label I'd loathed would work for the glory of God.

Just as the worst of Rahab's story drew me in and offered me hope, the worst in my story was doing the same for others. My story welcomed the hurting. It pulled up a chair to those who were scared to show their own labels. And it said, "Me too. I understand." The goal wasn't vulnerability. The goal wasn't to boast in our messes or sin. The goal was Christ and the hope we have only in Him.

FALSE TITLES

Rahab the harlot. Autumn the divorcée. In the days of old and today, your definition is wrapped up in titles. And all of us bear one, if not many. Think about it. When you are introduced to someone, people usually say, "This is so and so," and then they follow with a reference to your occupation or position or past accomplishments. Perhaps with something like, ". . . and he works at Walmart," ". . . and she is a doctor," or maybe ". . . and she is a stay-at-home mom." The description following your name is given in an effort to bring context to who you are. And it immediately describes us to someone, whether we realize it or not. Whether we like it or not.

But what if your title, like mine, is a negative one? Those don't typically serve as our introductions. But when we're not around, people refer to us by them. "You know Autumn? She is the pastor's daughter who divorced at twenty-two" or "You know so-and-so? He's been addicted to pain meds since his accident" or "You know so-and-so? She's had an abortion."

Are you even aware of the titles you have? Or, like a tag stitched inside the collar of a shirt, have you minimized, ignored, or felt embarrassed by the less-than-holy label inside your heart? An unaddressed title still marks you. It manipulates you and bosses you around. It messes with your mind and may be the reason you respond the way you do when certain opportunities arise, even if you don't realize it.

Whatever title you bear, it is not greater than the one God has given you. God wants you to be known by the "title" he has given you: "So in Christ Jesus you are all children of God through faith" (Galatians 3:26 NIV). If Satan can dominate you with the worthless or demeaning titles of the world, you've diminished the power of the cross of Jesus Christ in your life. Satan will claim glory for terrorizing your life while you live in the nightmare.

We must redirect the focus of our personal definitions. Those with a past know exactly what I am talking about. We must define our thoughts by the truth of God's Word and not by the fleeting, judgmental, hurtful titles of the world. When we hear the tender title *child of God*, it brings with it a sense of belonging, not rejection. It is acceptance despite our imperfections. When we train our minds to resonate with who God says we are, the ugly, painful, sinful titles become, as my dad said, "something God has brought us through."

Is there something in your life that you feel you'll never get through? What has defined you as "less than"? Can you imagine being free from it? It's hard to live above definitions we have earned. But when we operate first under titles less than *child of God*, we set ourselves up for disservice or detriment or, worse, bondage. This is exactly where Satan wants to keep us, tagged by a defective title— degrading our worth and crippling our effectiveness. Satan wants to stop you. God wants to empower you.

In the end, Satan stops us when we accept any humanistic titles; when we believe that is all we will ever become. It's time to be set free. How do we do this? Frankly, it's not as hard as we make it.

First, we simply need to identify our titles as being in disagreement with what it means to be God's children. Second, we need to shift our thoughts to believe what God says, not what the world says or what we think about ourselves. John 1:12 says, "Yet to all who did receive [Christ], to those who believed in his name, he gave the right to become children of God" (NIV). When we repent of our sins and accept Christ as Lord, we are saved and adopted as his children. Consider the ways we are defined as God's children.

1. Our debts are covered and our sins are no longer held against us (Galatians 4:4–7; 2 Corinthians 5:19).

2. We are God's heirs, part of the family (Romans 8:16–17), with an unshakeable inheritance (1 Peter 1:3–5).

3. We are cared for by God, both physically and emotionally, and lack no good thing in him (Psalm 8:4; Matthew 10:30–31; Psalm 84:11).

4. We have astounding authority and power (Ephesians 6:13–17; Romans 8:31, 35–39).

5. We have the mind of Christ (1 Corinthians 2:16).

6. We are free (Romans 6:14; 1 John 3:6; Galatians 2:20).

7. We have an extraordinary purpose and are meant to do good works (Jeremiah 29:11; Ephesians 2:10; John 15:8).

8. We are beautiful, and God takes delight in us (Psalm 139:13–16; Zephaniah 3:17).

As we explore our titles, you can't argue with these truths. If your title does not align with Scripture, it is false. And I believe false definitions of self fall into two categories: publicly assigned and self-given ones.

Publicly Assigned Titles

Publicly assigned titles arise in a myriad of ways and can be negative or positive in nature. Let's talk about the negative side first. Maybe you have earned a critical title in the eyes of the public, as Rahab and I did. This kind of title is almost always rooted in something we *did*, whether true or not. The options are seemingly endless: gossiper, liar, adulterer, bad mother, or addict to name just a few. Wherever you go, you are plagued by this definition. And such a negative publicly assigned tag gnaws, irritates, and weighs heavily on you.

Conversely, there are also positive publicly assigned titles. For example, devoted parent, business owner, award winner, diligent worker, or gifted teacher are commendable labels. They are rewarding, encouraging, and supporting. Sometimes the problem with positive titles, however, is that they may lead us toward pride and entitlement. Unlike the negative publicly assigned titles we want to hide, we're proud to wear positive ones on the outside of our lives, like a designer label depicting status, power, or wealth.

My friend, these positive titles can affect us just as adversely as the negative ones. If even the best of titles have a greater influence on how you operate than the titles given to you by the God of this universe, you are robbed. They will not work on your behalf like the ones with the force of God behind them. As great as your college graduate status is, for instance, it is not as great as being God's child. The titles of *good mom* or *great wife* are incredible yet still fleeting. If we try to live up to these titles we may miss the most important title to focus on: *ambassador for Jesus.* I challenge you not to be too caught up in anything that would replace that title. I do not want you to focus on the good thing and bypass the God thing. Pause for a moment and consider the positive titles you have in your life. How much security do you put in them?

You can still be proud of a title and not prideful about it, but that requires an understanding of the One who gave you the ability to earn the title in the first place. Otherwise, it can create just as much bondage over our hearts as harlotry can. The day we love our positive title too much is the day God could take it away. God is after connection with us, and when a positive title becomes a god to which we sacrifice and obsessively devote ourselves, we are worshipping it and not him.

We must not put too much in our earthly titles. They are something we have done or currently do, not the person we were created to be. Let me be perfectly clear: that title you value will eventually lead you to bondage. I find Satan in the pride we take in the titles we bear. He wants you to value something that you will never live up to. A "perfect parent" has never existed. A "perfect marriage" is a lie. It isn't a thing. Trying to achieve the reality of these titles will leave you frustrated with huge feelings of inadequacy. Titles can be a trap set by Satan to compete with the Lord in your life. Don't drink the Kool-Aid. Don't buy the lie.

Self-Given Titles

Likely subtler in nature than the overt titles the public assigns to us are self-given titles. These are what you have believed about yourself. No one may know these titles; you keep them to yourself. Nevertheless, they hold you back. These titles are more dangerous to you than the ones you bear publicly. They are lies Satan has convinced you of: unlovable, overlooked, worthless, stupid, etc. Sure, someone may look at you and think you have it going on. But in the back of your mind, all you can think is, *If they only knew who I really am.*

Though the self-given titles are more secret in nature, our behavior rises from them. You are a product of your thinking. Proverbs 23:7 says, "For as he thinks within himself, so he is." What are the thoughts you think toward yourself?

* * *

Whether your title is publicly assigned or self-given, positive or negative in nature, these titles need to be identified and evaluated with the help of the Holy Spirit. And they should be challenged when they do not agree with all it means to be a child of God. Not just challenged but destroyed. As 2 Corinthians 10:5 puts it: "We are destroying speculations and every lofty thing raised up against the knowledge of God, and we are taking every thought captive to the obedience of Christ." This happens *not* with mere positive thinking but by the power of God and his Word. Come walk the road of polished palace floors and dusty rocky terrain to see how one man's life was challenged in such a way.

WHEN GOD DECLARES YOUR TITLE

The Bible introduces Moses as a Hebrew baby whose life was protected from a death sentence. To evade the Egyptian king's order to kill all Hebrew male babies, Moses's mother hid him in a basket and placed him in a river. Pharaoh's daughter rescued him from the waters of death, was moved to pity, and took him home (Exodus 2:1–6, 10).

Moses, thus, grew up in Pharaoh's household at a time when Egypt was at the height of its power. Acts 7:22 says he "was educated in all the wisdom of the Egyptians and was powerful in speech and action" (NIV). He accessed the best and was honored by the public for his knowledge, military training,[4] and position. We can surmise he was held in high regard. Publicly assigned labels were undoubtedly projected onto him.

Moving forward in the story, the duality of Moses's labels came to a head. He was raised and trained as an Egyptian. Yet he also understood he was born a Hebrew. Those were his true people. While out walking one day, the scene of a physical clash exposed his mental one. He saw an Egyptian strike a Hebrew slave, and in a protective response, Moses struck the Egyptian dead. When he realized others had seen what he had done, Moses fled to the land of Midian and became a shepherd for a man named Jethro (Exodus 2:11–3:1).

Moses pastured the flock of Jethro for forty years. He went from honorable living arrangements and prestigious training to handling smelly sheep day in and day out. I wonder what titles, if any, Moses gave himself during this period. I wonder which ones from his time in Egypt he questioned as a result of being in this place. What must it have been like not to operate in the titles the Egyptians publicly assigned to him?

In the midst of the monotonous directing of sheep in a mountainous region, in a powerful visual display, God appeared to Moses in a burning bush. That's right. God entered the scene, reaching out to the murderer who had fled and become a shepherd. In Exodus 3:10, God commissioned Moses: "Therefore, come now, and I will send you to Pharaoh, so that you may bring My people, the sons of Israel, out of Egypt." Moses replied with an incriminating statement. "But Moses said to God, 'Who am I, that I should go to Pharaoh, and that I should bring the sons of Israel out of Egypt?'" (v. 11).

God clearly stated Moses was the guy to do a miraculous task for him. God would not have asked this of just anyone, but because of how Moses defined himself, true or not, he literally questioned his God-given purpose—questioned it of God himself. We don't know if Moses's response was rooted in a false sense of insignificance or an appropriate realization of his nothingness apart from God, but we do know it was not the truth about him when he stood in the presence of the Almighty.

"And God said, 'I will be with you. And this will be the sign to you that it is I who have sent you: When you have brought the people out of Egypt, you will worship God on this mountain'" (Exodus 3:12 NIV). In this holy exchange, God spoke truth to Moses about his purpose, thus speaking to who he was—a deliverer who would be accompanied by the presence of God. Identity was set in the context of relationship once again.

God saw a competent, prepared vessel to complete the task as deliverer and his words didn't indicate anything less. But Moses was faced with a choice. Receive and believe by faith he could do what God called him to do and be the person God already defined him as . . . or turn his face from burning glory back to smelly sheep.

An infant decreed to be murdered turned adopted prince. Then a murderer turned lowly shepherd. Talk about the weight of public titles. And, finally, Moses became a mighty deliverer, prophet, and man who dwelled before the Almighty. Talk about the freedom of God-given titles.

RETITLED

In an effort to sanitize a woman God created to reside in the bloodline of Jesus, some have suggested Rahab's name be translated "innkeeper" based on the word's Hebrew consonants. While there is some validity to this, it excludes other textual support for her label to remain "harlot," such as the New Testament references (Hebrews 11:31; James 2:25).[5] The relabeling didn't work. At the end of the day, she was a harlot, and God was determined to use her.

We don't need to cover up our ugly with something to soften the sin; it's futile. Our best efforts to clean ourselves up, minimize titles to be socially acceptable, or argue away their intensity will never come close to what God can do.

He takes the old and makes it new. He redeems and turns our story around for the miraculous. Rahab the harlot turned Rahab the hero. And then there's me, the divorcée who found a life of fearlessness and freedom when I understood the power of the title Jesus died to give me.

While I operate under that one powerful title every day, the lesser titles in my life change, so I experience new ones in natural ways. And though many of them are great, I want *all* God has to offer in the supernatural. I want him to see me as someone who doesn't take pride in a specific title, but rather takes pride in him and in him alone.

His limitless power shattered my mental chains. And I was freed in my thinking to do impossible things because God saw me as more. Second Corinthians 5:21 says, "He made Him who knew no sin to be sin on our behalf, so that we might become the righteousness of God in Him." He looked at me and saw his Son, Jesus.

• • •

I went away for a weekend by myself last year. I do this at the beginning of every year. Just me and Jesus. During this time, I pray and seek his face on what he wants for the year and of me. A number of colossal things weighed on me as a leader last year, and I landed at the beach heavier than the dragging pull of the tide. As soon as I sat in my rental car, the weight of the titles I bear—CEO, radio host, author—all seemed to hit so hard. I lost it. I cried all the way to the hotel simply because of their crushing weight. When I pulled into the parking lot, the Holy Spirit spoke so clearly to me, "Autumn, you are not any of those things to me. This weekend you are just Autumn, my child." All of a sudden the overwhelming weight of responsibility left and peace set in to my weary spirit. When I got the titles of the world out of the way, my Father God could minister to me even more deeply.

Sweet reader, there is much freedom in knowing Who defines you. As a believer, *child of God* is the only label worthy of defining who you are. I dare you to live titled by anything less. Truly, "how great a love the Father has bestowed on us, that we would be called children of God; and such we are" (1 John 3:1).

Chapter Three

———•••———

I AM NOT
ONE SEASON

My best friend and I walked quickly one November evening into a beautiful, outdoor, upscale, artsy shopping area adorned with the whimsical lights and scents of the season. For weeks she'd insisted repeatedly that we visit the lobby of a ritzy hotel to see the decor, which was a weird yet reasonable request. She was quiet and seemed nervous as we walked, but before I could ask what her deal was, I entered the lobby of this most fancy hotel. I paused to take in the splendor of the scene, but I was interrupted when one of my boyfriend's friends emerged from the shadows and handed me an armful of two dozen roses.

Completely shocked, I greeted him and asked where he came from and why he was giving me roses. It was to no avail. He wouldn't answer me but only smiled and pointed in a forward motion for me to walk farther. My heart started beating so fast. I knew something was up. Next I found myself standing face to face with my sister, who had also suddenly emerged. She handed me another two dozen roses and motioned me to keep walking forward. She wouldn't answer any of my questions either. Even when I annoyingly repeated them several times, she simply said, "Move forward."

As I continued, my brother greeted me next; he, too, came from out of nowhere. He held two dozen roses and refused to answer any of my questions. He simply pointed me on. I was walking so fast at this point I was practically running. I knew my Eddie Miles was waiting for me somewhere to ask me the long-awaited, big question. My entourage and I walked several more yards, and I could see a small crowd gathered ahead in the distance. They all seemed to be staring at me, smiling, but I couldn't see anything else. I asked my posse, "Is this for me?" Again, *crickets.* They simply smiled and pointed ahead, as was their routine, and I walked even faster. (Clearly they all knew me well and my tenacity to get to the bottom of any situation.)

As I approached the crowd of people, I saw Eddie wearing a black suit and holding four dozen roses. He looked so good, even though he was shaking and sweating nervously. He stood beside a bench draped in tulle with candles surrounding him in a large shape of a heart. (Insert heart-eyed emoji.) He grabbed my hand, sat me down, and began washing my feet. It was freezing because of the November temperature, but I didn't care. This was the moment I had waited for my entire life. He then took out his journal, which was filled with notes that he had written to me every day for the last year. He opened it to the last entry and read its closing words— the question I had dreamed about: "Will you marry me?" Speechless, I paused, and then shouted and cried yes. With one yes, my season had finally changed. I was no longer "Autumn, the girl who got divorced." I was now "Autumn, the girl engaged to Eddie Miles."

DRYING FLAX

The story of Rahab is extremely intriguing, but it's even more riveting to watch the hand of God work in every single detail of her story as her seasons changed. Let me offer you a fair warning: I'm going to geek out on you in this chapter. We get a glimpse of the beautiful way Rahab was divinely positioned when we consider the season of the events. God does not exclude the natural rhythms of this earthly life in the ways he fulfills his plans.

The season in which the spies went to Jericho was after the city's flax was harvested and laid out to dry. The timing is important because without the harvest of the flax, there would have been no covering for the spies to hide under. Recall the scene: "But the woman had taken the two men and hidden them, and she said, 'Yes, the men came to me, but I did not know where they were from.' . . . But she had brought them up to the roof and hidden them in the stalks of flax which she had laid in order on the roof" (Joshua 2:4, 6).

According to my study, flax was dried on the rooftops exposed to the elements. The hand of God was so involved; he positioned Rahab on a specific side of the wall of Jericho because he knew drying flax would be there too. I will go into the weighty specifics of her location in a later chapter, but it is important to note her home was covered by one of the rooftops used to dry the flax. Both her location and the season were pivotal to the story. If it had been spring, fall, or winter, she and the spies may have been killed. Where could they have hidden from the guards? Research tells us these stalks were about two feet tall.[6] Undoubtedly, the guards thought there was no way to hide two grown men in two-feet-high plants set out to dry. They moved along because of this assumption coupled with Rahab's lie about the spies' whereabouts.

The strategy on God's part moves me. Rahab had not known

how important the flax harvest or her role in it would be. The planting, growing, and harvesting of those stalks would save her life and the lives of an entire nation. I wonder if the flax was even an incredible annoyance to her at times. I mean, she had flax on her roof for an undisclosed amount of time! That would drive anyone crazy. I don't even like dishes in my kitchen sink for one day. But God knew that the location of her rooftop, coupled with the season, would ultimately lead to her own harvest. He did not have only the protection of the spies in mind, but also the ransoming of Rahab and her family.

We talk about seasons in general so much in our Christian culture, but there are several things accompanying seasons almost always left out. Every season is strategic from God's point of view. We need to appreciate each one of them, even the hard ones. Rahab has given us a powerful example of what to do with a season. Her story depicts God as a God of seasons.

YOU CANNOT SKIP A SEASON

Let's convo first about the order of seasons. Mommies of young kiddos, single people, and entrepreneurs who are about to rip your hair out, listen up. Hard seasons are just as beneficial and, most of the time, more profitable than good ones. I wish it weren't that way, but it is. There is no short cut to the goodness of God promised to you.

He is good, and in his goodness he has designed things in your life to make you, not break you. One season will build on the other. They are layered, interrelated, and dependent. Without the preparation of the soil, there would be no proper sowing season. Without the sowing season, there would be no growing season. Without the pruning season, no healthy growth. Without the healthy growth, no abundant harvest season. We often want to throw out a season or two and move full steam ahead to harvest, failing to consider the necessity of the intermediary steps. In nature, full sowing and reaping include the following steps: soil preparation, sowing, growth, pruning, harvest, and utilization. Each step or season is fixed and vital to the harvest.

The planting season takes work. First, you must prepare the soil, till the soil, and fertilize the soil. Taking care of the soil itself is a whole season. Then when you have prepared the way with a good foundation and you are confident of God's leading, you plant. After you have planted a seed, it needs constant supervision. The seed must be cared for and not abandoned. It must be given the ultimate TLC. With time, you will see a tiny sprout. Nourishment and protection and even pruning will facilitate a harvest.

Now that we all have a degree in agriculture, let's move forward.

Our seasons align with the supernatural ordering of God's directed paths. What you don't realize, friends, is the parallel growth of both the thing planted and you yourself. Not only does *it* grow, whatever it may be; you grow, too, during seasons of life when you let them have their proper way. Skipping a season would be detrimental to your harvest season.

You are not made up of one season. Thank God each season serves a purpose in your life, be it a season of tilling shallow soil, a season of trials, or a season of persevering in sowing. Your depth and character are made in both the good seasons and the tough ones. As we consider the overall rhythm of sowing and reaping, we must be confident of Christ's words in John 15:8: "By this my Father is glorified, that you bear much fruit" (ESV). Each season works together to bring a harvest. The harvest won't come if one is omitted.

HANDS IN THE DIRT

Soil preparation sets the flaxseed up for success. Flax tolerates a range of climates, but the surface of the soil should be a smooth, fine-textured seedbed, firm enough to avoid large air pockets. Plowing, furrowing, and harrowing are all agricultural steps used in the beginning to prepare the soil for cultivation. It's a lot of work!

The condition of the soil sets the context for everything following. It dictates how and when the seed should be sown. It influences the growth and nourishment of the seed into a sprout. It is the context for a harvest.

But we overlook it. We avoid it. We don't want to stoop down, reach our clean hands into the rough soil of life, and dig the needed furrow for seed. Without the season of preparing the soil, you'll have no flax. No harvest. You'll forfeit the costly seed.

Once I had my life-altering encounter with the Lord that morning at three o'clock, I knew I was different, completely changed on the inside, yet none of my circumstances had been altered. I believed in Jesus and knew he was real, but that was about it. I had a ton of work to do. I was still in a bad marriage and still had many obstacles to overcome. Nothing was magically different. I had to do the work with the help of the Lord to dig myself out of the mess I had made. I started at the very beginning. For once in my life I saw myself for who I really was spiritually— a baby believer— and stopped believing the lies that I was feeding everyone else. Although I'd attended church my entire life, I had never actually chosen to fully believe in Jesus and live by faith. So that is where my spiritual work began.

I could feel God wanting to do something amazing with me, but he had more faith in me than I had in him. I had to build it little by little. I remember for the first time praying as if God was actually in my car. I prayed out loud even though it felt so weird, but at that point God was all I had. He was my everything. Though still in the captivity of my first marriage, I was growing wildly in my prayer life. The Lord began revealing to me that faith would be a big deal in my life. I knew I would need to exercise it where God was calling me, so I began asking the Lord to show himself to me. With my prayer life very active, I would ask God to do things for me such as provide me with a twenty-dollar tip at a specific table I was waiting on (which was a lot back then), and he would do it.

The Lord and I became friends, and I began to draw my confidence from him. Months passed, and I began to notice my speech was different. The things I was saying were grace-based rather than discouragement-based. I watched my fear begin to deteriorate. I became bold in how I spoke to my then husband. He noticed my courage that was coming from my stability in the Lord. Things did not change overnight for me, but that 3:00 a.m. transformation made it possible to do the challenging work of tilling the hard ground of my life and prepping the soil for a fruitful ministry. Those days, although difficult, are the very reason I can do ministry today. The work of prepping my soil has begun to pay off.

If you're in the soil-preparation season, don't be afraid to get your hands a little dirty. Maximize it, for the sowing will not be a waste if you do.

SOWING SEED

The sowing season feels like the hardest of all the seasons. You are constantly working. You get tired. There is no harvest in sight. It's kind of a thankless season, but an important one. We seem to think the harvest season is the most important one, but without a season of sowing seed correctly, there would be no hope for a harvest.

And He spoke many things to them in parables, saying, "Behold, the sower went out to sow; and as he sowed, some seeds fell beside the road, and the birds came and ate them up. Others fell on the rocky places, where they did not have much soil; and immediately they sprang up, because they had no depth of soil. But when the sun had risen, they were scorched; and because they had no root, they withered away. Others fell among the thorns, and the thorns came up and choked them out. And others fell on the good soil and yielded a crop, some a hundredfold, some sixty, and some thirty." (Matthew 13:3–8)

The parable of the sower is premised on the condition of the soil and speaks not only to the seasons of sowing and reaping, but also speaks indirectly of the in-between seasons. Let's break it down verse by verse to capture the principles entailed in a harvest.

In verse 4, we see the sower planting seed in sowing season. Either out of casual tossing or sloppiness, he wasted some of the seed. He threw it in a place that would not produce, beside the road where constant steps made a hardened path. No seed merely lying on the surface of packed dirt can take root. Flax, when it is sown properly, should be planted a quarter inch to one-half inch deep. I told you I would geek out. Sure, it's not much, but it's more than sitting on top of dirt! This casually viewed seed was lost to the birds. The sower forfeited some of his harvest because he wasn't careful with all of his seed. He was sloppy.

Sometimes we can get lazy when sowing. We just want the seed sown and start throwing it everywhere without actually placing the seed where it can grow. When we do this, we miss opportunity. For instance, I think of church plants and any ministry in the infant stages. Too often in today's age we allow a lie about impressing others to dictate our ministry choices. Did we tell everyone on social media we are doing something great for God? Does everyone know we're taking a huge step of faith? How do our print media and images for marketing look? Do they look cool enough? Will they be impressive? If we are more concerned about what others think of us than giving full attention to the people we are leading, we can end up losing our flock because we are unintentional, distracted, or sloppy. The seed takes root not because of any fancy print media but by loving on people and showing them the gospel. When we get it twisted, thinking that ministry is about something other than people and caring for them, we waste the seed.

Matthew 13:19 says, "When anyone hears the word of the kingdom and does not understand it, the evil one comes and snatches away what has been sown in his heart. This is the one on whom seed was sown beside the road." How does this make you reconsider the way you sow and the condition of the soil—especially in a ministry context? Do you really take time with the one "seed," trusting God to help him or her understand God's truths? We must be intentional about each seed, especially those who have hard hearts. A lazy sower will not reach those whose hearts are hard. You must be "faithful in a very little thing" to be "faithful also in much" (Luke 16:10).

No matter the size of what it is you are investing in, vocational ministry or not, care for the one individual. For me, when God prompts my spirit about a member of my team, I follow through. Most of the time when I reach out, that person will begin to cry or tell me how much prayer was needed that day. Be intentional to the woman in your small group, or the dad at school, or the kid who is always alone and never seems to have a parent with him. Pour some intentionality into them. Do not be focused so much on growth and being noticed that you do not care for the seeds God gives you directly. Don't be sloppy, rushing ahead for more, or you will lose some harvest.

NO ROOTS

"Others fell on the rocky places, where they did not have much soil; and immediately they sprang up, because they had no depth of soil.

But when the sun had risen, they were scorched; and because they had no root, they withered away" (Matthew 13:5–6).

Verses 5 and 6 continue to remind us why the soil is so important. We are also indirectly introduced to the concept of the care and time required for a seed to take root. The sower forfeited his harvest again here because the soil was too shallow for roots to develop.

No sprout of flax can withstand the natural elements of wind and rain if there are no roots. It is the same for you and me. We can lack roots because we're sowing in soil not properly prepared; it's too shallow. Or the soil may be deep enough, but not enough time has passed for the roots to develop. Seasons of waiting and growth must be part of the process for a lasting harvest.

Let me speak to those who planted quickly. Maybe you rushed into a relationship or even a marriage, and now you realize your roots are shallow or maybe nonexistent. Maybe you rushed to buy a house before realizing you couldn't actually afford it. Or you hurried and got pregnant and now the baby is here and it is overwhelming you. Perhaps it's a business deal you hastily invested in and now, uh-oh, the reality of the decision you made is hitting you. The heat is on, and you are feeling it.

I prayed for ten years before God opened the door to my ministry. I thought I was going die. I got frustrated with God some days, I would complain about the wait some days, I would cry some days, and some days I actually had faith and believed that God was going to do it. Back then I thought that ten years was a long time, but now I see the value in the soil of my heart, tilled and filled by prayer and waiting. It was the context for depth. It was a divine setup for my personal growth and the growth of the ministry to have proper, healthy roots. If I'd forced the ministry to develop on my timetable (which I really wanted to do), we would have lacked the depth of maturity needed to handle the trials and carry the weight of the vision. My haste and pure tenacity could've brought a harvest, but it wouldn't have lasted. I hadn't been ready for the season.

It is so vital to learn the value in the season of preparation and the season of waiting for things to take root. If you don't, whatever is sown will fall away "when affliction or persecution arises" because it has no root (Matthew 13:21). You must also actually give time to grow. If our seed seasons last more than a week or month, we are tempted to lose hope and ultimately even question whether God will produce anything out of them. I wonder how many God-authored seeds have been planted yet given up on too quickly. Growth of the flax took around three months.

Don't rush what God is asking of you. Satan will tell you that quicker is better, but the seed on top of the soil will perish because it didn't get deep enough to sprout roots. Quicker is not better.

Ultimately, roots must reach deep into our lives if they are going to bear any eternal fruit. In Colossians 2:7, Paul tells us we have "been firmly rooted" and are "being built up in Him and established in [our] faith." We don't have to risk the winds of trials blowing us away when our roots are firmly planted.

GROWING PAINS

Thus far we've looked at the importance of the seasons of soil preparation, waiting, and growth. There is still more before the harvest season, though. The parable of the sower continues in verse 7: "Others fell among the thorns, and the thorns came up and choked them out." Jesus explains this verse perfectly. (Of course he does! Insert praise hands emoji.) "And the one on whom seed was sown among the thorns, this is the man who hears the word, and the worry of the world and the deceitfulness of wealth choke the word, and it becomes unfruitful" (Matthew 13:22).

Thorns have an aggressive growth habit, wrapping around plants, even piercing them, and eventually cutting off their nutrient supply. I couldn't better describe how worry and the obsession of money choke the life out of us. The impact of thorns stands in stark contrast to what may also feel painful at first, but is for our benefit—the pruning of the master Gardener. When God trims and cuts, his actions give life not death: "Every branch that bears fruit, He prunes it so that it may bear more fruit" (John 15:2). Out of love, he cuts the useless shoots that would otherwise burden and steal from the growth.

This one gets to me as a mom of four precious treasures, as I'm sure it does for any parent—especially those with kids under the age of eighteen. Jesus talks about the worries of the world choking out the seed, rendering it unfruitful. If there is ever a time to fight against worldliness, it's today. The world is dying to snatch up our children, and Satan wants to claim them as his. We cannot conform. We cannot care more about what the world thinks about our parenting than about how our parenting will influence the hearts of our kids. We must be gangster in how we view our parenting.

A few days ago, my daughter's middle school held an assembly about internet safety. She'd begged us in the past for social media, but her dad and I had said no without hesitation. We knew she wasn't ready for the responsibility of saying no to some of its temptations. But when she walked in the door after school that day, she sat down and said, "Mom, they taught us about pornography and how to stay away from it." She continued, saying, "Do you know what sexting is? Why would anyone do that?" I was ready to cry for the world we live in, but when I was about to answer, she said, "Mom, thank you for saying no to my request for social media. I don't think I am ready for it yet." And with that, the Lord encouraged me more deeply than she will ever know.

Point your children to the cross. Say the hard things. Don't be scared of the moms group peer pressure to do what everyone else is doing. Teach your kids how to obey. Don't be their friends; they have enough of them. They need a mama and a daddy to train them so one day they'll be prepared to be mamas and daddies themselves, warriors crushing the places of darkness with light.

We must partner with God through prayer, discipline, and trust to remove the "useless shoots" of the ways of this world. Don't let the thorns render you or your children, your literal seed, unfruitful. Fight for them.

SEASON OF HARVEST

Matthew 13:8 ends with the sower planting seed among the good soil. When they went through the growing season, they "yielded a crop, some hundredfold, some sixty, and some thirty." I'd be happy with any of those!

Those only came because no season was skipped. Those came because of tilled soil, root development, waiting, pruning, nourishment, and more waiting. Matthew 13:23 provides really cool insight to the harvest: "And the one on whom seed was sown on the good soil, this is the man who hears the word and understands it." It is a biblical principle of reaping and sowing. A heart receptive of the seed of the gospel will bear fruit.

Faith executed will breed a harvest season. Flax is ready to harvest approximately one hundred days after sowing. When the stalks are about two feet high, they are pulled up and allowed to dry first for a time in the field. Then they are soaked for several weeks and allowed to dry again for a much longer period of time—about two years.[7] Two whole years involved in the harvest season! It was most likely during this second, longer drying period where we encounter Rahab and the spies. The flax was there drying on her roof as part of the extended harvest season.

The flax is significant to me because as I read this passage over and over, I couldn't help but think about all of the seasons Rahab endured to get to where she was—standing on a roof of abundant harvest. An innocent little girl to a citywide known harlot. A pagan idolater to a believer. A nobody to a somebody. Her harvest is still producing as I write this book about her. How could she have known the hard seasons would produce a harvest that would last throughout the centuries?

The key to her harvest season was God at the center of it. She believed he was able to do what he said he would do. The key to our harvest season will be the same. John 12:24 says that "unless a grain of wheat falls to the earth and dies, it remains alone; but if it dies, it bears much fruit." The seed reaches its full and proper development by being sown in the ground and dying; this requires faith by the sower. So, too, the death of Christ was a sowing for a greater harvest. In him, we die to ourselves and gain a new life. The growing pains are worth it.

• • •

In the last several years, I have become extremely thankful for my prior seasons, specifically my abusive first marriage and the repercussion of being kicked out of my church. At the time this was horrifying. A nightmare come true. It hurt every ounce of me, to my very core. I still bear the emotional scars of those seasons.

But then God came in to do what he does. He began to work through it, bringing an astonishing harvest. I've been able to speak on TV and radio shows. I've shared articles in op-eds for the *Washington Post*, Religion News Service, *Christianity Today*, and many others on behalf of abuse victims and my ministry. I've looked hurt church members in the face and apologized on behalf of the ones inflicting pain. I've been able to relate to people in a way I don't think I ever would have if my soul had not been bruised so badly.

Rather than allowing the pain of this world to choke the life out of me or letting doubt sway me during the rocky seasons, I aligned myself with the One I know to be trustworthy. I have experienced the true and raw grace of God, who is good even when I am not.

APPLYING THE HARVEST

Your harvest isn't just about you. Rahab's definitely was not. She put her harvest to use and was deliberate with the flax. She quickly made a decision about hiding the spies because she saw an opportunity and got creative. She worked with what she had and didn't miss out because of what she lacked.

If Rahab hadn't, both she and the spies would have died. She was smart and quick on her feet. She wasn't properly educated, but she leveraged her work and life experience. She had people skills and knew how to deal with men. Her past season benefited her present.

People often ask me what my Bible degree is in. My answer leaves them stumped. "I have a degree in the travel industry," I respond. I did attend two years of Bible college and have taken many related courses since then, but I always get weird looks—and further questions—when I tell them about my educational background.

I can say I have learned more about the Bible during my Bible time the past twenty years than some degree holders would say they did during a year of study. I use what I have, and what I have is the Word to study every day. I also believe my lack of a formal Bible degree while doing what I do every day has challenged me to study all the harder. Knowing where God has placed me, I know I need to study as much as possible to offer depth and insight into God's Word. Sometimes lacking something will benefit you the most. I have applied what I know to steward the harvest.

As God gives you a harvest season, be sure your perspective is right. Without question, the harvest will bless you, but it may also crush you if you aren't focused on Jesus. The harvest of your life isn't meant purely for you.

HANDLING THE HARVEST

You want the harvest season. You dream of it. You desperately desire the season of work, waiting, and pruning to be over. But did you realize the harvest season is more work than the planting and growing season? Your harvest may crush you under its weight if you don't prepare for it.

I used to watch a show about lottery winners. It showcased their journeys after the big wins. Interestingly, some are in jail or homeless. Some have spent all their money on frivolous things. And, worse, others have been murdered for their money. As I watched, I knew exactly why. The harvest came too soon, and they didn't know how to handle it. They didn't plan for it because they weren't expecting it. The harvest caught them off guard, and it destroyed them. Only a heart prepared by the experience and lessons from the prior seasons can handle the harvest season.

As Rahab and the flax process demonstrate, there is still work in the harvest season. Remember, the entire process for harvesting flax lasts approximately two years. After the lengthy drying time, the flax is then beaten, scraped, and combed to remove the outer covering and pulp. This leaves the fibers clean and ready to be spun for linen production.

What will you do with your harvest? How will it be managed? Where will you put it? Who will take care of it? If we are being honest with ourselves, we may not be ready for the harvest. Be patient with the seasons of your life because they prepare you with wisdom for the abundance of the harvest.

Chapter Four

I AM LISTENING

In an earlier chapter, I mentioned that I go to the beach for an annual prayer retreat every January. The beach is a good friend of mine. It's my happy place and stirs my passions and creativity. It is a beautiful backdrop, displaying God's might. I often say God lives at the beach, even though I know he is everywhere. But it's one of the places I connect best with him.

When I went in 2016, the weather was nasty, cold, and drizzly the entire time. The beach was deserted, mirroring the way I felt on the inside. Though I was facing the hope of a new year with an expectant spirit of what God could do, I couldn't shake a feeling of dread. In the previous year, God had overwhelmed me with his goodness, both personally through the adoption of our two youngest babies, as well as in my ministry with its incredible growth. I had all the reason in the world to be joyful, but I felt horrible instead.

Every morning at the beach I took a walk and prayed. I prayed for my personal needs and the needs of my ministry staff. Then I shifted gears and prayed for the ministry as a whole. I laid out my personal goals and dreams before God and sought his dreams and plans, especially over things like any directional changes we needed to make or people we needed to hire. Historically, this weekend prayer retreat is when God has given me a word of the year for our ministry.

On this visit, during a morning walk of prayer, I found myself close to the pier, several condo buildings away from where I was staying. I was wearing my candy-apple red, thickly lined jacket with the hood up over my head, pulled tight to protect my hair from drizzle. The waves roared, and as they slammed the shoreline they left a most concerning dirty foam. With the temperature somewhere around forty-five degrees, it was miserable.

I decided to head back to my condo and escape the weather conditions when the Holy Spirit spoke loudly to me and boldly proclaimed, "Shift and shed." I immediately stopped. All of a sudden I wasn't so frustrated about the weather. I was captivated by the bold words of the Spirit.

My mind started racing as I prayed for clarity on what the words meant. Trying to add my own clarification, I began to wonder what needed to "shift" and what needed to be "shed" in our ministry. The words felt somewhat alarming. It seemed almost like a "prepare yourself" message. For a moment, I felt like I could resonate with Jeremiah the prophet. He delivered hard, even unwelcome messages to the nation of Israel. He was called the "weeping prophet" because he empathized and ached so greatly for the people and felt the weight of prophetic hardship. This, too, felt deep. But at the time I didn't know what it meant.

I anticipated that 2016 wasn't going to be easy, but I also knew a loving God was preparing my spirit for what was about to take place. Feeling fearful as I stood and walked back to my condo, God began to speak again. He spoke such comfort with things like, "I am moving this year" and "I will be with you the entire year" and "follow me completely." I chose to remain confident in him no matter what unfolded.

I returned to a team anxiously waiting to hear all God spoke to me on my prayer retreat. Calmly but convincingly I shared the unmistakable message to them. One by one, "shift and shed" resonated with them. We didn't know what God was going to do, but we knew he was in control whatever happened.

• • •

I began to sense God telling me it was time to shift the ministry to a different focus. Not a different mission per se, just a different focus—be it the ministry taking on a new look or even a new name. But the words the Holy Spirit spoke within me were meant for something more than a mere external change. They were all-encompassing and would pierce our hearts and souls, calling us continually back to God for our true life and vision.

Just a few short months after my beach trip, "shift and shed" began to unfold before us in a tangible way. One of our beloved staff members was diagnosed with brain cancer, and it ultimately claimed her life not long after the initial diagnosis. I was back at the same beach for a short vacation when I received the devastatingly hard call. Later in the same year, we experienced a season of pruning and betrayal by someone we never imagined would turn against us. By December 2016, I couldn't wait for it to be 2017. It was undoubtedly the toughest ministry year of my life. Satan tried to do a number on us, and I was left grieving a dear team member and healing from some other deep wounds.

But in his love, God had prepared us for it all when he spoke those challenging words to me. I listened and received them, trusting God to be the author of my days and the Good Shepherd to lead me. His Spirit comforted us on the painful, hard days when I wanted to know the why behind the shifting and the shedding. It was one of the most trying years, but it was also one of the years God spoke to us the loudest. Or maybe we *heard* God the clearest because we believed he had a word for us. His presence was more powerful in my life than ever as I leaned in close for his voice and desperately depended on his every word.

A HEART TO HEAR

Rahab's courageous choice to hide the spies was in part because she'd heard of the Lord's reputation. The God of Abraham was powerful. When he said he was going to do something, he always followed through. Rahab couldn't deny the results of the God of Israel. His faithfulness stood in complete contrast to the pagan gods the people of Jericho worshipped.

> Now before the men lay down, she came up to them on the roof, and said to the men, "I know that the LORD has given you the land, and that the terror of you has fallen on us, and that all the inhabitants of the land have melted away before you. For we have heard how the LORD dried up the water of the Red Sea before you when you came out of Egypt, and what you did to the two kings of the Amorites who were beyond the Jordan, to Sihon and Og, whom you utterly destroyed. When we heard it, our hearts melted and no courage remained in any man any longer because of you; for the LORD your God, he is God in heaven above and on earth beneath. (Joshua 2:8–11)

One of the most important things Rahab did was listen to the stories of God. These stories stirred and challenged her heart in such a way that change followed. She didn't just hear about God; she believed in God because of her choice to consciously listen to the stories. The stories about God produced her belief in God. This was key to Rahab's actions.

What if Rahab hadn't listened? She could have casually listened and chalked it up to a good story, but she didn't. One thing is for sure, this book would not exist if that were the case. She responded to the information given, and it saved her life. I'll argue that it *gave* her life.

For years growing up I heard about God. In church I was taught every Bible story you could think of. I heard all the time about how God wanted to speak to me. "Read your Bible," my Sunday school teacher would say encouragingly. "God wants to talk to you," my parents would say. But to be totally honest, I didn't have a clue about what God sounded like or even how to talk to him. I was told to pray, but it felt ridiculous because it seemed like I was talking to no one. I wanted to hear from God, sure, but the idea of it actually happening seemed weird.

Every story I heard about him stirred my interest, but my response stopped there. I heard but didn't listen. Not until that time at three in the morning when God spoke so clearly to me from his Word did I really tune in. And like Rahab, it *gave* me life. It was the first time I truly quieted myself to listen. Before that night, I would have argued that I had been listening to the voice of God, but in reality I had been confused about the difference between hearing and listening.

●　●　●

It's easy to confuse hearing with listening. Although you have to hear to listen, you do not have to listen to hear. Hearing is simply our ears sensing sound vibrations. Listening engages the brain to understand what those sound vibrations mean. When we begin to listen with our brains, we can do things with the information, such as believe and make decisions based on our interpretations. Our hearts and souls become involved.

I give you this tiny physiology lesson to make you think and to ask a question: Have you been simply hearing information about God, or have you been listening to God?

Our churches are bloated with individuals who believe they know God when, in reality, they have only heard about him. They are intellectually fat but spiritually malnourished. They have *heard*, but they have never responded. They haven't discerned that the information was for them.

When it comes to the things of God, it is not enough to know about God. We must listen to what he says to us, coming to *know* and *hear* him for ourselves. Just as Rahab's life was radically transformed when she listened to his truth, yours can be too. When we listen, we experience the one true living God. He separates himself from every lifeless idol and pagan god because he is the God who is alive and who speaks to us. I don't want to miss any of his words.

• • •

God speaks, but do you listen? I guarantee you are listening to something. The world is screaming at you to listen to it. From podcasts, to social media, to text messages, to email, to your calendar, to your DVR, the world screams. Satan laughs when we allow the clutter of this world to fill our minds and stifle God's voice. He knows our greatest resource is listening to the Spirit of God and the Word of God, so he tries to cover them up. He tries to drown them out. And too easily, he does.

With God as our Father, we are designed and purposed to hear from God. In the Old Testament, the Israelites were often identified as a people who could hear God. Time and time again, God commanded them to listen. In Deuteronomy 6:4, he said, "Hear, O Israel! The LORD is our God, the LORD is one!" The Hebrew word for "hear" in this passage, *shema,* means "to hear intelligently, often with implication of attention, obedience, etc."[8] This word begins the most important prayer in Judaism still prayed today. There is overwhelming significance when you are marked by the ability to hear from the holy all-powerful God.

To hear from God is both a privilege and a command. It carries a divine weight of response. If you are having trouble hearing from God, it could be because of the noise around you. It could be because, as was once true for me, you have never tried to listen to God for yourself and have confused hearing and listening. Or it could be because you didn't know he desires to speak to you individually. How can we hear his voice?

THE WAYS HE SPEAKS

I go on a prayer retreat every year not because I'm super spiritual but because I have to shut everything down to listen. Listening to the voice of God has been the greatest asset to my life. Just like Rahab's choice to listen and respond helped save her life, it has done the same for mine. Maybe you want to listen, but you wonder how to do so. God speaking so clearly to me in those early-morning hours helped me realize how I best hear God. I started learning what to look for and what to listen for. I disciplined myself to learn his voice.

For a while, I focused on what spoke to me most and what his voice sounded like in my spirit. His voice to me was less of a hearing experience and more of a knowing. It was something I knew and felt sure of in my spirit. When I quieted myself and focused on him, I could listen to what he was trying to say to me. Over the years, it has become the one thing for which I yearn. When I listen to God's voice, I feel seen, known, and understood by my heavenly Father.

I have a raw and active relationship with him because it's not a one-sided conversation. I shut my mouth and listen! I know whatever he is saying is for me directly and is for my good. It must be obeyed, heeded, and acted upon.

John 10:27 says, "My sheep hear My voice, and I know them, and they follow Me." It doesn't say his sheep should or could hear his voice. It says they do! God wants you to listen to him. If you are a believer, he takes up residence in you. It's not enough for you to simply know *of* him. He wants you to know his voice. He wants to produce in you what is only possible by knowledge he possesses. So, in what ways do we hear the voice of God?

God speaks to us in several ways. According to Psalm 19:1, he speaks to us through nature: "The heavens declare the glory of God; the skies proclaim the work of his hands" (NIV). Apart from nature itself, where I feel God moving in my spirit, especially at the beach, he also speaks to us through his Word and his Spirit. Let's look further at how we hear God and encounter him specifically through these two primary ways.

THE SPIRIT

John 16:13–14 tells us about the role of the Spirit of God: "But when He, the Spirit of truth, comes, He will guide you into all the truth; for He will not speak on His own initiative, but whatever He hears, He will speak; and He will disclose to you what is to come. He will glorify Me, for He will take of Mine and will disclose it to you."

The Spirit's job is to guide you in all truth. In truth he will comfort, counsel, make intercession for us in our prayer, convict us of sin, and ultimately guide us where God has purposed for us to go. If you think about it, each of these ways is a way we hear the voice of God. The Spirit is multifaceted, wondrous, miraculous, and, in my opinion, the most disrespected person of the Trinity. He is the greatest resource we have as Christians. If we listen to the Spirit of God, we encounter God.

When the Holy Spirit told me "shift and shed" back in January of 2016, I froze in my tracks because I knew God was going to do exactly what he said. The Spirit of God was speaking to where he would guide me. I could have very well dismissed what I heard, but because I listened, I was able to stand when the shifting and shedding process began. It was a *shema* moment; my attention, intention, and obedience were involved in the hearing.

• • •

Do you ever have an overwhelming sense of yes in your spirit about something or someone? Oftentimes this is the Spirit of God speaking to you. Many times we shrug off these yeses in our spirit and we don't do anything about them. But we are meant to listen with a heart bent toward response.

I clearly remember sitting at my dining room table one night at nine when the Spirit of God said, "Email the radio station." I knew God was giving me a passion for radio and media but did not know how to get into it. I didn't have a background in radio, but I really liked it.

I had been a guest on a show in Dallas several times and loved the host of the show. In response to the Spirit's words, I emailed the station manager, who immediately replied. Only a few weeks later, I became the cohost of the show, which has since led to my own daily radio show. The Spirit was guiding me, revealing God's purpose for me. I listened, and a door was opened.

On the contrary, the Spirit's directing us can also involve a no or a closed door. Do you ever have a check or a bad feeling in your spirit about something or someone? This is oftentimes the Spirit of God warning you about a specific direction or association. When God says no, it's not because he's mean or wants to withhold from you, but because he has a greater yes coming your way. If we don't heed the no, destruction or disappointment may be on the other end. Don't try to manipulate your way around it. Listen to it. Submit to it.

When it comes to hearing God through his Spirit, it is also important to remember the voice of God is meant for more than our individual benefit. For example, have you ever been thinking about someone and felt prompted to check on him or her? The Spirit of God often alerts us to care for someone through prayer, encouragement, a word of faith, a display of mercy, provision, or more.

We hired a new precious intern for the ministry not long ago. God laid her on my heart so incredibly strong one day as I was leaving my house. I didn't have her phone number because she was so new with us, but I knew the Lord was telling me to pray for her and to check in on her right then. I contacted a team member to get her number so I could call. She didn't answer, but I left her a message. Hours later, we found out the grocery store in which she worked was getting robbed at the exact time I'd called her. She was being held at gunpoint! God alerted my spirit to great concern for my precious team member. She was terribly shaken up but okay.

Just as with Rahab, listening saves us from certain things God does not want us to experience. It also propels us into crazy, amazing futures. And it benefits those around us. It reveals who God is by teaching us his ways. We are meant to encounter God through the voice of his Spirit. American evangelist D. L. Moody said it well: "You might as well try to hear without ears or breathe without lungs, as try to live a Christian life without the Spirit of God in your heart."

THE WORD

The Word of God is my best friend. Is it weird to know I even sleep beside it some days? There have been times when I have put my copy of God's Word under my pillow and slept well because of the comfort it brings me. It is my rock. It is my active counsel. It confirms my steps. "For the word of God is living and active and sharper than any two-edged sword, and piercing as far as the division of soul and spirit, of both joints and marrow, and able to judge the thoughts and intentions of the heart" (Hebrews 4:12).

Scripture gives me peace and direction. It is my treasure. Ever since the Lord spoke so directly to me at three in the morning using my blue Bible, my life has never been the same. I was contemplating ending my life and was petrified of death when I read those life-giving words: "the righteous will have long life."

The living Word gave me life when I was lifeless. It resurrected my spirit from my grave of depression. It pierced the darkness of my soul and brought light. It stood with me when all had forsaken me. It comforted me with promises when all I had received were nos. Through all betrayals and blessing, it has carried me.

The Word of God speaks, but we must come to it with a humility and expectancy, taking its pages as the very Word of the living, active, awesome God. We must listen to it with our hearts. When we internalize the powerful words from its divine pages, we are inhaling the very breath of God. It is the Script and Blueprint for all areas of our lives. To not use it is to deprive yourself of the greatest gift given to humanity—a full relationship with God, who gave up everything to have a relationship with us. "In the beginning was the Word, and the Word was with God, and the Word was God. All things came into being through Him. . . . In Him was life, and the life was the Light of men" (John 1:1–4).

Practically speaking, I encourage you to read the Bible regularly. As you read, in order to truly listen, silence all distractions and ask the Spirit of God to reveal what you need to hear. When a passage grabs your attention, pause and listen. Ask the Holy Spirit to reveal why it pulls at your heart. Observe what the passage says. Consider its meaning. Ask what it reveals about God. And lastly, ask him to help you understand how it applies to you. Some say the Bible is irrelevant—to them, I say it changes my life every day.

Hearing the voice of God through his Word does not need to be difficult. If we discipline ourselves and take the time to read it, we *will* hear God's voice. God's Word and Spirit often work in tandem with one another. For instance, the night I heard the Lord speak to me, his Spirit asked me, "Do you remember?" The knowing and sense of familiarity in my spirit prompted me to get out of my bed and grab my Bible.

Romans 8:16 says, "The Spirit Himself testifies with our spirit that we are children of God." Though this verse talks specifically about the Spirit confirming our identity as children of God, another verse shows the Spirit also moves in extended matters. Paul, in Romans 9:1, says, "I am telling the truth in Christ, I am not lying, my conscious testifies with me in the Holy Spirit." In short, the Spirit bears witness to what is true. The Spirit illuminates the Word of God for you as you read!

• • •

Because the Word of God is so powerful, Satan attacks God's Word by disarming God's people. It's hard to find people who read and study the Bible on a daily basis. Other things crowd the lives of Christians, and they attempt to live the Christian life without the resources they need to do it. We have become biblically illiterate as a church, relying on books and podcasts to supplement the truth and depth of wisdom that only the Word of God can bring. We accept hand-me-down revelations about God from teachers and friends rather than entering into the presence of the living God ourselves and hearing him speak.

I have spoken for many years on the biblical illiteracy problem. It's a sore spot for me because I know it's an area of weakness in our churches. I heard recently of a young man who had been discipled by his pastor for fifteen years. The pastor, who loves the Word of God, discovered the mentee didn't believe the Bible was the inspired Word of God. Instead, he judged it as just another self-help book. When I heard this story, my eyes welled with tears. This mentality is utter deception and a lie from Satan. To consider God's Word a self-help book, as though it were no different from the book I am writing, is blasphemous. It's nauseating. How many lies from Satan that sounded like truth had this guy believed before he finally got to a point where he thought the Bible had no power.

Second Timothy 3:16–17 puts it like this: "All Scripture is inspired by God and profitable for teaching, for reproof, for correction, for training in righteousness; so that the man of God may be adequate, equipped for every good work." When I hear stories like the one above, I know evil has taken root. The Word of God wants to equip us for the things we face and draw us closer to God. There is no excuse not to hear from him. Though his Word was written centuries ago, his Spirit is alive and active within us. He has spoken and is still speaking. It's our privilege and responsibility to quiet ourselves to listen.

● ● ●

In Luke 9:35, Jesus is transfigured right before Peter, James, and John. God speaks to them and says, "This is my Son, whom I have chosen; listen to him" (NIV). Can you even imagine it? What God commands them to do on behalf of his Son is to *listen* to him. Because God knows true listening—*shema*—involves intention and the will of the heart. It involves obedience and a response. It calls forth relationship and love.

There is so much to gain from listening to the Lord. Rahab listened, and it changed her life. Her active listening and her obedient response are still changing lives today. Commit to listen to the Lord God, specifically through his Spirit living inside of you and his living Word. He is speaking even now and has something to say to you. Ask the Lord to reveal what he wants for you, and ask him to show an entirely new side of himself to you.

Chapter Five

I AM RISK

The rain pattered hard against the church windows that Sunday morning. The sound almost drowned out the scruff of shoes as the deacons took the stage of our small church. My dad had served as pastor there since 1986. It'd been our home for nearly two decades.

Back in 2002, a storm of risk descended upon my parents with such intensity that every area of their lives was exposed to the elements, especially their church life. My pending divorce and my parents' choice to stand with me in it was the setup for those tempestuous times. Because of their role in the church, their public stance was inevitably viewed with heightened judgment and weight. After searching the Scriptures and the wealth of wisdom therein, they stood as the steel support beam, with me and for me, sustaining the weak structure of my life. The context for a bitter battle in our church about abuse and divorce was set. The storm was brewing.

They chose me, their daughter, over man's opinion. They risked everything to align themselves with the truth of God's Word and to obey him. As pastor of the church, longevity notwithstanding, my dad and consequentially my mom risked their salary, stability, and reputation in the community. If risk is understood as "the possibility of loss or injury,"[9] then my parents risked everything for me.

Two years later in June 2004, I found the storm winds were quieter. I had just married the love of my life, Eddie Miles, and was walking in the epitome of God's grace. While the consequences of the divorce had largely subsided for me, externally speaking, it was a different story for my parents. They were in the thick of reaping the consequences of their obedience to God. Their risk proved to be catastrophic and unspeakably costly when they professed their support of me.

As the rain came down that Sunday morning, the deacons stood close together in an effort to show some sort of unity. They read their meticulously typed letter to the congregation my dad had shepherded tirelessly over the past twenty years. My dad sat with my mom while the letter was read. They both silently endured the insults of its contents, hurled like lightning, piercing their hearts. The letter concluded by announcing a forced resignation for my dad. This church and his passion were snatched out from under him because he and my mom had stood for what was right.

When the deacons finished reading the letter, an abnormally loud crash of thunder bellowed in the sanctuary, as if God groaned and mourned in anger. Cries of shock filled the room as the congregation began to process the disturbing conclusion to my dad's years of service. From the accounts of those in attendance, something evil seemed to have taken over. One member even stated, "The work of Satan has been done here. Mark the doors 'Ichabod'" (see 1 Samuel 4:21). The departure of God's glory from Israel in the days of Samuel was his reference. It sure felt dark. Dad and Mom were asked to leave and not come back, even for one more Sunday. No "thank you." No sending party. Nothing.

When the storm winds of risk slammed the church doors shut on my parents, they did not slam shut the goodness of God. Substantial favor and blessing followed them in concrete ways soon after. Despite the devastation, God did not leave them in lack. He restored what was lost, as he had done for Job in the Scriptures. God increased their influence and favor because they decided to side with him.

RISK LIKE RAHAB

And the king of Jericho sent word to Rahab, saying, "Bring out the men who have come to you, who have entered your house, for they have come to search out all the land." But the woman had taken the two men and hidden them, and she said, "Yes, the men came to me, but I did not know where they were from." (Joshua 2:3–4)

Now then, please swear to me by the LORD that you will show kindness to my family, because I have shown kindness to you. Give me a sure sign that you will spare the lives of my father and mother, my brothers and sisters, and all who belong to them—and that you will save us from death. (vv. 12–13 NIV)

Knock. Knock. Knock! I wonder if Rahab felt the urgent pounding on the door in her heart, too, as it raced faster with adrenaline. This time her door opened and swayed heavily inside for a reason different from normal. Surely the king's men's very presence felt intimidating. Maybe even enough to make her cave and change her mind. Would the enemy intimidate her enough to let fear win? In that moment, her very life hung in the balance.

No doubt Satan uses great intimidation as a tactic to destroy God's plans and us in the process. He "prowls around like a roaring lion" (1 Peter 5:8). On that spring day in Jericho, it seems the roaring lion's schemes looked a lot like king's men dressed in armor, questioning a scandalous woman of society. Though not omniscient and still subservient to the eternal plans of God, the enemy seeks to oppose God in every way. What God is for, Satan is against. He knew if Rahab risked everything for Israel and the God of Israel, he would lose the battle.

But there in her doorway, outnumbered and accused, risk greeted Rahab for the second time. Hiding the spies in the first place was a risk. Now would she risk further and lie to the king's men? She knew about the Israelites' plan to take the city of Jericho by force, which would mean certain death for her. She was already a walking dead woman. It was treason to harbor the Israelite spies. If she didn't risk and face the tactics of her enemy, she would die, and so would all of her family. Risking her life at the very moment she was questioned was worth it if it meant God could intervene.

Satan knew there would be a reward for her risk because God rewards faith. And this time the reward was a big one. It would mean the fulfillment of the promise for Israel. Maybe Rahab dreamed of being saved by the God of Israel she'd heard such amazing things about. But she wasn't only saved. The outcome of Rahab's risk helped make victory possible for the Israelites and still encourages millions of people generations later.

Rahab was no longer a dead woman walking. Her risk aligned her with the same power of God that was legendary throughout Jericho. She certainly could not out risk the reward of God.

THE RISK OF SIGHT

I was on our elliptical machine one day just gliding away to my favorite jam when Eddie walked into the room. His look concerned me enough to stop and give him my undivided attention. He said calmly, "I think God wants me to quit my job, and I don't think God wants me to look for another job right now." Shocked, I said, "Huh?" He repeated the sentiment. We had two kids and bills to pay. Obeying the call felt steep, terrifying even, but he did. We took the risk. We did not risk just for the fun of it. We risked because God told us to.

Crazily, God provided us an opportunity that blessed us financially more than we could have imagined one month later. It paid us more money than we had ever made. The opportunity God provided allowed Eddie to join the staff of the Blush Network and helped it to get off the ground.

If we had gone by what we saw, like the bank statements and the list of bills we had with two kids and a mortgage, we never would have surrendered to the ask. What we saw should have made us cling to Eddie's current job as if every mouth to feed depended on it, because they did. But there was more at stake for us in the unseen. God provided via the currency of our faith and our risk.

We think faith is risky, but exercising it is the safest thing we can ever do. Faith cares not for the practical, temporal concerns, but begs us to go deeper because there is something greater than the practical things we see. I am not saying go quit your job and live on faith. We didn't place our faith in faith; we placed our faith in the words God spoke to Eddie.

Second Corinthians 5:7 says, "For we walk by faith, not by sight." Most people are inclined to do the opposite—to walk by sight and not by faith. When we live only by what we see and what makes sense to us, we forfeit God's power in our lives. Risk, this faith-based act of daring greatly, is pivotal to the supernatural processes of God. Want to see more of the hand of God? Then you must risk when he says to. You must step when he says step. You must believe even when he asks the ridiculous. His wisdom is unrivaled. You are not smarter or wiser than his leading. He won't be reckless with you. He has planned perfectly for your step, just like he planned for Rahab's.

Most of the things God asks us to do don't make sense at all in the physical world. Like at all. But the unknown that we struggle with is not unknown to the Lord. He is not dangerous. Let the grounding truth of the Bible be your vision. Psalm 119:105 says, "Your word is a lamp to my feet and a light to my path."

We don't need to have faith in faith; we are to have faith in God. "Biblical faith is not a vague hope grounded in imaginary, wishful thinking . . . biblical faith is not blind trust in the face of contrary evidence; rather, biblical faith is a confident trust in the eternal God who is all powerful, infinitely wise, eternally trustworthy."[10] He has a plan for the faith you exercise. Your faith without an objective of your faith will yield you nothing.

Living by what you see is the weightier risk if you ask me. Living by what you see interrupts the miraculous from knocking at your door. Living by what you see isn't a life of faith. Living by what you see breeds a boring, powerless life. We can risk when God calls us to step out in faith, fixing our eyes on the unseen, because we know Jesus, who is the "image of the invisible God" (Colossians 1:15).

COMFORT, THE ENEMY OF RISK

I recently heard about a woman who quit a well-paying job. Want to know why she quit? God told her to risk her finances and trust him. She obeyed, but right when she quit, she was bullied by her adult colleagues. One of them said, "Even if God did tell me to quit, I couldn't give up the money. It's too good." As I listened to the recount of the story, I got mad. A righteous anger swelled in me. "Really? Are you kidding me?" I immediately said. The bullying colleague bought the lie that money holds a greater reward than obedience to God. The power or temporal security of money was greater to her than God's provision on the other side of risk. Her comfortable lifestyle blinded her to the benefit of obedience to God. The verse in Romans 1:25 rang in my mind: "They exchanged the truth of God for a lie." Ugh! Satan took pleasure in that colleague. She sold what could be for what was. Another potential Rahab bites the dust. Another abundant life rejected. And for what? Something as fleeting as money. There are far more riches available than money.

Comfort is the great enemy of risk for God. It stands as one of the biggest reasons we are risk avoidant. Comfort incarcerates risk and steals your chance to reap the rewards. Comfort *can* be a blessing. It's not a bad thing in and of itself. Comfort is a cup of coffee first thing in the morning. But it's also another unnecessary pill to numb emotional pain. Comfort is a nice bowl of cookie dough ice cream (or at least mine is). It's also a work promotion, where the money feels good, but the toll it took on your family to climb the ladder is ignored. Comfort is trust in God. But it's also trust in your intellect or man's favor rather than in the ultimate Giver of those things. Comfort is an idol we worship in place of God all the while using the excuse of wisdom. In our limited intellect, we can render the God-appointed risk as irresponsible, but when we do, Satan cheers. He knows the trap he set for you has been successful.

God wants to give us more, and one of the ways he does so is through things that comfort. God gives us tangible comforts in our material possessions, our healthy bodies, great spouses, the blessing of children, friendships, and more. The problem comes when we're more comfortable with our comforts than with the Comforter. The problem comes when finite comforts keep us as "dead women walking" and stifled in our faith—as Rahab was prior to the arrival of the spies. We can be so unsure of who God is, we don't step out if it messes with our comfort. When we avoid risk, fear wins and we are disqualified from God's intended more.

Some of the wealthiest people I know refuse to be comfortable in the Lord first. Their tangible comforts usurp true, genuine comfort. When *things* make us stop seeking God and we rely on them to bring counterfeit comfort, we are in disastrous territory. Think about it. When we have nothing and are uncomfortable, it's easy to cry out to God to work on our behalf. We have nothing to lose! It's when God begins to give us what we ask for that we need to be aware of our comfort source.

If you're turning down the privilege to risk, ask yourself why. If we aren't careful, complacency creeps in. Before we know it, we are far from God, deceptively *too* satisfied with earthly comforts. Matthew 19:24 says, "Again I say to you, it is easier for a camel to go through the eye of a needle, than for a rich man to enter the kingdom of God." Jesus knows that once we seem to have everything the world has to offer in riches, we won't seek him as much.

Check in with God. If you are slipping, repent and ask forgiveness, and then move back into a place of risk for the Lord.

PERSPECTIVE

You may wonder how to risk. I want you to take it one step at a time and with the right perspective. Don't focus on what you could lose by risking in faith. Nor obsess on what could be ahead, because we don't truly know. It is of paramount importance that we focus on Jesus. If we look at Rahab's risk, she recounted who God was, aligned herself with this truth, and surrendered in faith. Sure, she recognized what was at stake and what could be. But her gaze had to ultimately be toward the One who could deliver her family.

Focus and perspective are imperative to our steps of risk. We must focus on who God is. We must keep a kingdom perspective. Why? Because we'll either be stagnate, risk-avoidant believers or we'll crash with disillusionment. What happens if you *don't* get the raise from work after sacrificially giving twenty dollars in the offering? What happens if you took the risk to start your own company after hearing from the Lord and three long, hard years have passed, and you're barely making ends meet? What happens when you risked vulnerability and reached out to someone, but the love hasn't been reciprocated, the forgiveness hasn't been extended, the acceptance hasn't been acknowledged? What then?

Did God fail you? Will your faith not be rewarded? We mustn't be so spiritually presumptuous as to assume a reward will follow our risk according to our ways and our timetable. The apostle Paul knew this well. His whole life was one risk after another. He was obedient to the call of God and always aimed to speak of the gospel, but he definitely didn't get what he always hoped for from his risk. For instance, "the Holy Spirit solemnly testifies to [him] in every city, saying that bonds and afflictions await [him]" (Acts 20:23). Doesn't feel like much of a reward for taking a risk to testify about the gospel, does it? While risking on behalf of God, he experienced "dangers from rivers, dangers from robbers, dangers from [his] countrymen, dangers from the Gentiles, dangers in the city, dangers in the wilderness, dangers on the sea . . . sleepless nights, [was] in hunger and thirst, often without food, in cold and exposure" (2 Corinthians 11:26–27). He didn't receive the VIP bunk with silk sheets on the boat sailing from Caesarea to Rome. Actually, he was a political prisoner and nearly shipwrecked. Major risk. Want another way he risked for God? He didn't have consistent, dependable income from fellow believers to support the ministry God appointed him to. He was a tentmaker, with his own "hands ministered to [his] necessities" (Acts 20:34 ESV). Paul was a man of risk.

Paul's reward was in Christ alone. His goal in risk taking wasn't the adrenaline rush. It wasn't to be a celebrity or have a million Instagram followers. It wasn't to *get* something specific from God. It was to advance the gospel. His objective was to know Christ. I'll let him say it in his own words: "But whatever things were gain to me, those things I have counted as loss for the sake of Christ. More than that, I count all things to be loss in view of the surpassing value of knowing Christ Jesus my Lord, for whom I have suffered the loss of all things . . . so that I may gain Christ" (Philippians 3:7–8).

He had nothing to lose and everything to gain. He risked one step at a time and received his reward in Jesus.

• • •

Risk for the Lord may seem insane, but I want you to understand risk from God's perspective. Risk is hard, but you gotta do it if you are going to experience more than you are now. Do you want more? Are you begging God to show himself mighty in your life? Are you tired of the same ol' thing and the same ol' day? Are you bored with your life? Have you lived your entire life without seeing God's power? If you say yes to any of these things, I'll guess you don't risk much for God. Here are some of the benefits when you get off the couch of comfort and do so:

- "A faithful man will abound with blessings" (Proverbs 28:20).
- "His lord said to him, 'Well done, good and faithful servant; you were faithful over a few things, I will make you ruler over many things'" (Matthew 25:21 NKJV).
- "So that the proof of your faith, being more precious than gold . . . may be found to result in praise and glory and honor at the revelation of Jesus Christ . . . obtaining as the outcome of your faith the salvation of your souls" (1 Peter 1:7–9).
- "Let us not lose heart in doing good, for in due time we will reap if we do not grow weary" (Galatians 6:9).

- "And without faith it is impossible to please Him, for he who comes to God must believe that He is and that He is a rewarder of those who seek Him" (Hebrews 11:6).

GOD'S QUESTIONABLE DECISION TO CHOOSE US

The story of risk on Rahab's part is admirable. However, the risk in Rahab's story was twofold. She risked, but was it not also risky when God gave Rahab the power to participate in the execution of his plan? Now let me add a caveat. God is omniscient and omnipotent, so at the end of the day, his ways will not fail. His Word will be accomplished if we drop the ball. But we get to work with him! Don't be sending me any crazy emails. This section is meant to challenge you.

Rahab stuck her neck out for the Lord. She risked everything, but she had to choose to do so. What about God, who is perfect, all-knowing, all-powerful, putting his plan into play for us to participate in? The very thought is shocking to me.

God did something scandalous in creating us. He gave us a free will to choose whether or not we wanted to participate in his plan. Meaning we do not have to if we don't want to. However, if you dare call yourself a Christian, you need to be representing Christ.

Our very lives carry the privileged weight of risk as made evident in 2 Corinthians 5:20: "Therefore, we are ambassadors for Christ, as though God were making an appeal through us." The verse continues, emphasizing the message our lives should represent so we can "be reconciled to God." I sit and stare at the words, "as though God were making an appeal through us." God literally chose us to make an appeal for him. He chose us, humanity, to carry out his objective for the world. We are his ambassadors, his megaphone, and his intercom system. He asks us to participate in the gospel, but will we? Is it that important to you? Is he? You get to choose whether you will risk or not.

Reality check. What are you living for? What life are you settling for? God called you out as an ambassador for him. Do you care? Will you operate like one? Are you stewarding this calling well?

The privilege to be called an ambassador for the Lord keeps me up at night. It drives me. I want to do everything possible for his name because of what he has done for me. The humility of understanding his might and my weakness creates such a deep honor for the God I serve. I want to steward well every calling he has given me, knowing I represent God himself. I don't want to talk myself out of what the Lord asks of me, but rather say yes to him. I want to see God move on my behalf, and if I have to sacrifice Autumn Miles's insecurity or comfort to do so, then so be it.

Take a minute and thank God for taking a risk on you. The eternal world is ready to support your step as you respond to God. You are his ambassador!

— • • • —

Following Christ demands risk. To not risk is to miss out on the fullness of life with him. Though risk can require payment of what seems secure, of what seems logical in front of us, and of earthly comforts, it's a low cost in exchange for the abundant life we are promised. I don't want us to miss the reward of the risk. I don't want us to miss him. Risk when he says to. Your blessing is waiting.

I leave you with the poem of a ten-year-old "Rahab" named Ana Puncochar. Let the words from this inspiring young woman challenge you to risk. I was blown away that at such a young age she is ready to risk. It was inspiring to my adult heart as I read her beautiful words, and I pray they inspire you as well.

WILL IT BE

Shall it always be in this world
Injust
Ignorance
To woman kind
Overpower
To male kind
Underestimate
To child kind

How can our pledge talk of justice for all
When this may never be a reality

If no being has will to step up to this
We will
Underestimated
Child

You may be brave
But only the bravest step up for what is right
Only the strongest admit that they too have weakness
These bravest
Are small
These strongest
Are short
But
These bravest
Are smart
These strongest
Are Brave

Smart enough not to pretend to be another
Brave enough
To not try to be anything
But themselves

If nobody stands up
We will
And we're not afraid to

So shall it be
That you stand
Or we stand
For liberty and equal rights for all
Man
woman
child

Chapter Six

• • •

I AM FLAWED

I was sitting in the large, musty-smelling, barely occupied detention hall room. Out of the corner of my eye, I could tell the boy
diagonal to me wanted to pass a note. The days of texting were not yet
a part of our reality. Ahh, the good ol' days.

I frequented the detention hall as a sophomore in high school.
School to me was 0 percent about learning and 100 percent about
people. If I had friends, I believed I was succeeding at school no
matter what the report card said. My parents wholeheartedly dis-
agreed with my mantra "Cs get degrees," and to this day roll their eyes
when I quote it. It still gets a rise out of them. They retort, "Autumn,
we always knew you were smarter than you let on." They are right,
but in high school, being smart wasn't my objective—it was having
fun and being awesome.

This particular day in detention I was actually serving *two* detentions. I was good at getting them. My teachers would warn me about
talking during class, and before you knew it, I'd not only receive one
detention but also another for every word I said after the initial warning. I think the school policy permitted for up to three detentions

to be issued in a single day. Or at least I assume so because it wasn't unusual for me to rack up three in a class period.

Per her norm, the detention hall teacher placed her desk behind us in an effort to best see what we were doing at all times. It didn't bother me one bit as a regular. I learned how to maneuver my body in such a way that she would never suspect me of passing notes during the thirty minutes of detention. And I was good at it—until this day. As I leaned over to grab the note from my friend's hand, I got busted. Mid-reach, the teacher sternly and loudly said my name. "Autumn Carey, please come back to my desk!" To this day, the memory of her harsh, convicting voice makes my skin crawl.

After the teacher called my name, I turned my head to say, "Coming." I was shocked to see my dad standing at her desk. He stared at me, but I held his gaze for only a second. Some twenty-two years later, this moment still haunts me.

Immediately, I felt myself become white as a sheet and started hyperventilating. I knew I was in trouble. The teacher continued, "Your dad would like to take you home." I gathered my things and bid farewell indefinitely to my detention buddies, walking slowly to the back of the detention hall. It was as though my feet were aware of the pending bondage I would face in a short time, and I struggled to move well.

I had been lying to my parents about my detentions for a while. Well, a long while, actually, because I'd never told them about a single one. Because I was involved in so many extracurricular activities, it was easy for me to come up with an excuse as to why I would be home late. I alternated excuses and told them things like, "I have to decorate the homecoming float" or "I have to hang posters in the school for student council." Most of the time these were actually true; I just failed to mention I served detention before any of them happened.

As I walked toward my dad, he said nothing. There was no smile to greet me. There was no hello. No twinkle in his baby blues. He looked at the teacher, thanked her for calling, and turned to leave while gesturing for me to follow. At this point, beads of sweat fell down my back as if I'd just completed a mile run in gym class. We finally got to "cruck," the endearing nickname for his truck because it was half car, half truck and resembled an El Camino. He opened my door for me in silence. When we got inside, he said, "Autumn, I came looking for you at the student council meeting you told me you were attending, but there wasn't one. When I asked the office where you could be, they suggested the detention hall."

Cut to me. I wanted to die. The cherry on top was when he said, "Autumn, I know how many detentions you've had, and I don't even know what to say. How does anyone get fifty-two detentions?" Embarrassed and horrified, I was caught red-handed. There was no excuse and absolutely no justification for what had happened. I'd lied a lot. And now I was caught. I had to pay the price for the lies. Liar, liar, pants on fire.

I'm thankful the Lord has since transformed my mind about lying. It is one of the things I absolutely detest most today and, ironically, the one thing for which my kids get most punished. It's also something my husband and I do not allow in our marriage. Even a "little white lie" isn't permitted.

Even if I remove lying from the equation, though, I am flawed. So very flawed. (Insert ghost horrified face emoji.) The more I get to know the Lord, the more I see how truly flawed I am. You are flawed too. Despite our flaws, the Lord purposes us for greatness and chooses us to participate with him. Follow the story of Rahab, flawed even in her attempt of obedience, and encounter a God whose mercy and faithfulness prevail greater than our sin.

WHITE LIES REMAIN LIES

Rahab's lies felt relatable. They were another thing I shared with her. We both obeyed God in significant ways, but not in every way. Let's look at the text in Joshua 2:4–5: "But [Rahab] had taken the two men and hidden them, and she said, 'Yes, the men came to me, but I did not know where they were from. It came about when it was time to shut the gate at dark, that the men went out; I do not know where the men went. Pursue them quickly, for you will overtake them.'"

When the guards showed up at Rahab's door, she was faced with a choice. She first lied when she acted as though she didn't know the spies were Israelites. She went on, lying a second time, when she chose to tell the guards the men had already left the city. She knew full well the spies were upstairs on her roof hidden in the harvested flax.

The author of the book of Joshua doesn't condone the lie nor judge it within the text. What does God say about it, though? According to number nine of the Ten Commandments, "You shall not bear false witness against your neighbor" (Exodus 20:16). In other words, do not lie. Do not speak falsely. God hates lying and sees it as an embodiment of the enemy, who stands in antithesis of truth, "because there is no truth in him . . . he is a liar and the father of lies" (John 8:44). We cannot sugarcoat Rahab's words. Her lie cannot be justified just because some may call it a "white lie." A white lie is still a lie. She sinned to save the spies.

Rahab's lie has made some steer clear of her story, particularly this portion. Things can get super messy when we try to reconcile the miracle God did for Rahab and the honor she is given when she lied outright. This chapter will no doubt make legalistic minds quiver in criticism, but I cannot write an entire book on Rahab and not confront her lie. She sinned but is still recognized for her faith in Hebrews 11. She lied but was still given in marriage to one of God's holy men.

I believe the Lord allowed the messiness to be included in the text to challenge us and teach us about his heart. While God would never approve a lie, he chose to work a miracle in spite of it.

———— • • • ————

Initially, it seems as though the lies of Rahab were rewarded. There is more going on here, though. I want to unpack what God may want us to gain by this story. Let's consider first how Rahab wasn't the only person in the Bible who lied and still gained the favor of God.

Let me draw your attention to Peter. After the Lord Jesus was arrested and taken away to the house of the high priest, the story goes back to Peter. Peter was warming his hands by a fire, likely lost in thought over what had just unraveled in his life. A servant girl in the courtyard called him out. Referring to his association with Jesus, she said, "This man was with him" (Luke 22:56 NIV). He denied it, saying, "Woman, I do not know Him" (v. 57). Two more times Peter denied knowing Jesus when questioned. Just hours earlier this passionate disciple had cut off a soldier's ear in order to protect Jesus, aligning himself with his Savior in every way possible.

Just as Rahab lied to save herself and the spies, Peter blatantly lied to save himself. Was he still the chosen vessel to start the church? Yes! Did the lie disqualify him? No! He was greatly flawed, but greatly used. He was a liar, yet anointed. How is this possible when the Word of God condemns lies?

Without a doubt, one of the reasons God left these two stories in the Bible is to highlight his heart. God sees our flawed, sinful actions through the righteousness of Christ. Because he is holy, he does indeed judge our sins; they most certainly do not go unpunished. Christ took the punishment for them on the cross shortly after Peter lied and betrayed him.

This is, in part, how we reconcile a holy God performing a miracle for a lying harlot. This is, in part, how we reconcile a righteous God entrusting his church to a disciple who didn't trust him enough to stand with him no matter what. Their imperfect stories highlight a perfect God who has covered us in grace. Their imperfect stories highlight a God who is faithful to keep his plans and graciously, mercifully allows us to participate in them.

As you consider Rahab's story, how do you identify? Since we are flawed, how do we walk out this Christian life knowing we screw up royally? How do we operate in the fullness we are promised in Christ but sin? How do we move forward when lying is the least of our flaws? Let's have a convo about it all. The roles of faith, forgiveness, grace, and presence are imperative if we want to conquer a life sidelined or even stopped by flaws.

FAITH WINS OVER FLAWS

Rahab was rewarded for her faith, not her lies. I believe this is another reason God left the story of Rahab in the Bible. In Hebrews 11, a Scripture segment often referred to as the "Hall of Faith," the Canaanite harlot is grouped with greats like Moses, Abraham, and Joseph. "By faith Rahab the harlot did not perish along with those who were disobedient, after she had welcomed the spies in peace" (v. 31). You know why she's included and esteemed as an example? Because of her faith. It wasn't because she aligned herself with God's vision and executed it flawlessly and without sin. She straight up sinned in the execution. But her faith was astounding. Her faith was life altering. Her faith highlighted the greatness of a God who is more merciful to us than we will ever be to ourselves. Her faith declared God was greater than any idol she ever served.

Her story is meant to serve as instruction, both in regard to her sin and her faith. Although this may be controversial to some church-goers, we've established Rahab's lie as a sin. And while we may not be known as liars, we are all sinners. Some type of sin tempts you on a regular basis. Maybe you serve God but are filled with self-serving motives. Maybe it's your heart posture, ugly with covert things like unforgiveness, raging jealousy, or unbelief. Maybe you find yourself struggling with judgment or pride. James smacks us in the face about the sin of judging others in James 4:10–12:

> Humble yourself in the presence of the Lord, and He will exalt you. Do not speak against one another, brethren. He who speaks against a brother or judges his brother, speaks against the law and judges the law; but if you judge the law, you are not a doer of the law but a judge of it. There is only one Lawgiver and Judge, the One who is able to save and to destroy; but who are you who judge your neighbor?

Just prior, in verse 6, he addresses pride: "God is opposed to the proud, but gives grace to the humble." Regardless of what feels relatable, we are sinners. Let's call it like it is.

But it doesn't end there. Sin doesn't win. Like Rahab, we do not "perish" in our sin. Faith always triumphs. Romans 5:1 says, "Therefore, having been justified by faith, we have peace with God through our Lord Jesus Christ." The Greek word for "justified" in this verse means to "render innocent."[11] Thus, no sin gets the final word in our lives. Our faith in Christ, coupled with our forgiveness in him, renders us justified, at peace with God, and innocent! Let's call ourselves like we *are*!

Rahab's faith rendered her righteous. Faith prevailed when the flaw was present. Isn't that great news? (Insert praise hands emoji.) The principle holds true for you too.

GOD DOESN'T DISQUALIFY YOU

We oftentimes highlight the flaw and disqualify the faith, but our God chooses over and over again to lavish grace upon a flawed life of faith. God didn't disqualify Rahab or Peter for their lies because his power was greater than the sin. His purposes are unhindered by our short-comings and limitations. He wasn't hindered by sin. He overcame it.

Flaws are the biggest things Satan uses to disqualify us from believing God can do amazing things through us. Satan will whisper, "You are too far gone." Or maybe he says, "God could never work through someone like you. God wants the good people." No, God wants the humble, willing, forgiven people. If sin disqualified us from God working through us and in us, God would use no one. The Bible says, "For all have sinned and fall short of the glory of God" (Romans 3:23).

Let me be clear. I am not condoning sin, but I do not condone sin keeping us from a vibrant walk with God either when he offers us grace. The rest of the sentence in Romans 3 is far too often left out when we quote it: "being justified as a gift by His grace through the redemption which is in Christ Jesus" (v. 24). There's the word of the hour—*justified*. Remember, those of us in Christ are rendered innocent. *Innocent!* What a God!

I am trying to help you if you believe you are too flawed to work for the Lord in any capacity. Every day I hear things like, "I don't talk to God anymore because I made some bad decisions and God is mad at me." Others will say, "Autumn, you don't understand what I have done. My sin is too big. I can't even believe God could work through me."

You have disqualified yourself when God never said you were disqualified. You have decided God's grace isn't enough. When we disqualify ourselves, we're basically hiding at home under pillows of false condemnation and a blanket of shame.

Paul says this about his sin: "For I know that nothing good dwells in me, that is, in my flesh; for the willing is present in me, but the doing of the good is not" (Romans 7:18). Here we even have Paul admitting he's so flawed, it's ridiculous. He's basically having a confession moment where it seems he bubbles over with conviction. He continues in further confession: "For the good that I want, I do not do, but I practice the very evil that I do not want. But if I am doing the very thing I do not want, I am no longer the one doing it, but the sin which dwells in me" (vv. 19–20).

Paul, the greatest missionary of all time, understood he was flawed badly. Rather than disqualifying himself from serving the Lord, he thanked God for the freedom he discovered in Jesus Christ, who forgave his flaws. Your problem is not your sin, although you need to repent from it. Your problem is the bondage the sin has on you. Your problem is acting as though the cross is less powerful than your sin. Your faulty belief system says your flaws are bigger than your faith. Sorry, that was harsh, but it's true. Second Corinthians 10:5 calls us to tear down those things that stand contrary to the truth of God: "We are destroying speculations and every lofty thing raised up against the knowledge of God, and we are taking every thought captive to the obedience of Christ."

Stop opting out of God's plans for you. Satan wants you to stay incarcerated. He wants you to dwell on your sin so that it defines you, robbing you of what God intends. God wants you to put your faith in him, and not to disqualify yourself when he hasn't.

FORGIVENESS WINS OVER FLAWS

Paul writes in Romans 6:1–2, "What shall we say then? Are we to continue in sin so that grace may increase? May it never be!" No doubt in our fallen, imperfect state, we will sin when trying to walk out our Christian life. This isn't an excuse to continue in sin. Nor is an ongoing struggle of sin the end all.

We must acknowledge our sin. If you have allowed sin to disqualify you from service to the Lord, it's time to have a good ol' confession session. Isaiah 55:7 says to "let him return to the LORD, and He will have compassion on him, and to our God, for He will abundantly pardon." God *abundantly* pardons.

Believer, the power of sin is broken! We are not perfect, but we are free from the dominion of sin. We are one with Christ, and no sin, shortcoming, or flaw has permission to be greater than his rule and way in our lives unless we allow it!

Also, when we *do* sin (because we will), we must get back up. I love this verse: "For a righteous man falls seven times, and rises again" (Proverbs 24:16). You fall once. You get back up. You fall again. You get back up. And it continues. He paid for it all on the cross. He died, was buried, and got back up for us. We now can get back up, too, for his forgiveness wins over our flaws.

GOD IS MORE GRACIOUS THAN MAN

Rahab has been judged throughout history for her lies. Religion is so judgmental. Even though God's rich mercy and Rahab's brave faith dignified her as a hero, she is still remembered as a harlot and liar. It can be the same with us.

Man has a propensity to be ferocious, condemning, and incredibly catty. You will be held in the boxes of your mistakes even if you've moved on in freedom. Social media makes this easy and, unfortunately, gives jerks, mean people, and losers a platform to air all their darkest, lowest thoughts about you. No one can maturely confront them when they're behind the protection of a screen. They are only screen brave. We are too often left to combat the judgment that barks louder than grace purely because of the constant accessibility of it.

Let me remind you—God's grace will overwhelm you when judgment from man seems to cripple you. God's grace is shocking and provocative to those who render themselves perfect. It offered a new start to the woman caught in the act of adultery. It dined with the tax collector who was known for over taxing the people. It even forgave a thief on the cross who deserved to die. His grace will never end with human capacity, for it is of a divine nature. King David knew this well. When he "sinned greatly," he pleaded, "Let us now fall into the hand of the LORD for His mercies are great, but do not let me fall into the hand of man" (2 Samuel 24:14).

Some of us still believe we should pay a penalty for sin because of what others say or the power we give sin. But it was paid in full when the Savior uttered, "It is finished" (John 19:30 NIV). Psalm 103:10–13 makes it clear: "He has not dealt with us according to our sins, nor rewarded us according to our iniquities. For as high as the heavens are above the earth, so great is His lovingkindness toward those who fear Him. As far as the east is from the west, so far has He removed our transgressions from us. Just as a father has compassion on his children, so the LORD has compassion on those who fear Him." God is gracious.

DO THE THING FLAWED

I can hear the wheels turning in your mind as you think of what *could* be if you were to step out in faith, in spite of your flaws or sin. Even when we confess sin, we will sin again. We are human, and the likelihood of never sinning again is not a reality. We have to step out in faith knowing we are flawed and act anyway. You have to do the thing flawed. Flawed individuals highlight the power, mercy, and faithfulness of God. He's all about his imperfect people doing the thing flawed; it showcases his perfection, might, and glory.

- Moses stuttered, but God asked him to speak before Pharaoh of Egypt for the release of his people.

- Gideon doubted God but became one of the greatest judges in Israel and a mighty warrior.
- David had an affair but was a man after God's own heart, chosen as the anointed king of Israel.

They did their things flawed. Paul said it best. When speaking about his own sins, he said, "Yet for this reason I found mercy, so that in me as the foremost, Jesus Christ might demonstrate His perfect patience as an example for those who would believe in Him for eternal life" (1 Timothy 1:16). We show up with our flaws and do the things God has asked of us. When we focus on the flaws, we are not focused on the all-sufficient God who paid for the flaws.

There has never been a day in my life I felt good enough to do what I do for a living. I am constantly aware of my need for a Savior to forgive me. If I focused too long on my shortcomings, I would never attempt anything for the Lord. Focus wins over flaws. My life, like Rahab's, proves it.

GOD DOESN'T WANT
"PERFECT PEOPLE"

I don't know about you, but I'd rather know I'm flawed and sinful than think I'm perfect. Perfectionism baits, trapping those who actually think they can achieve it. You know the grind if you struggle with this. You must have the perfect house, perfect Instagram account, perfect hair, perfect answers to everything, perfectly behaved kids, etc. Nothing can be out of place. Nothing can be flawed.

Satan whispers to us in such a way we actually believe we can achieve some level of perfection. Yet he also knows the only perfect human was Jesus Christ. If he can get us running after something we can never possibly achieve, we'll stay busy and remain in bondage while trying to hide our imperfections, insecurities, and flaws.

What's worse is the accompanying sin of self-righteousness so often associated with perfectionism.

We see God clearly and harshly rebuke the Pharisees and Sadducees for their self-righteousness. They may have done everything according to the law, but in doing things so perfectly, they forgot the heart of the law. Jesus called them "whitewashed tombs" (Matthew 23:27). He was sickened by the pride in their hearts, produced by their "perfect" actions.

God will never look for the perfect human, because he knows he only created one—his Son, Jesus. God looks for willing people whose hearts are flawed but are his. Second Chronicles 16:9 speaks beautifully of God's tenacity for such people: "For the eyes of the LORD move to and fro throughout the earth that He may strongly support those whose heart is completely His."

To those who admit they are sin sick, there is deliverance through the Savior. To those who obey despite their flaws, God enables (Philippians 2:13). Those who don't judgmentally snub their noses at present-day Rahabs have honored Christ (Matthew 25:40–45). The imperfect, flawed one is the perfect one for rescue.

— • • • —

I pray you are encouraged after reading this chapter. The flaws we have do not disqualify us when we surrender them to our Savior. I pray you are strengthened in your pursuit of what God could do through you, with you, and for you. Every Bible story, excluding those of Jesus, includes a flawed human working with a perfect God. Remember, he chose Rahab flawed; he has also chosen you. It is by faith, as a forgiven child of God, that you show up to do the things he has called you to do. God always uses flawed, willing people.

Chapter Seven

I AM SACRIFICE

It was freezing outside on February 20, 2015. A huge "ice apoca-lypse" was forecasted for the next two days, and Eddie and I sped, as fast as we could, from Dallas to Houston. We were headed to the hospital to pick up our newly adopted son, Moses. A two-and-a-half-year wait was finally coming to an end. The last three days were a whirlwind of activity I couldn't forget if my life depended on it.

That morning, unbeknownst to me, I sat having my sweet, per-fectly mixed coffee for the last time in about a year. I stared out the window, leisurely enjoying the morning so much I had to remind myself my coffee was getting cold and needed drinking. My Bible was laid out before me. I was going in and out of prayer for the child promised to us not forty-eight hours before. I couldn't concen-trate on prayer. I couldn't concentrate on the Bible. All I could think about was the child God promised us.

My phone rang and broke my concentration. The voice on the other end was calm yet firm. "She is in labor; make your way to Houston," our adoption representative said. I jumped up and tripped over the mountain of blue baby boy paraphernalia scattered in our living room. I did not know how to respond, so I began frantically pacing. I asked in shock, "Okay, what do I do?" She repeated, "Come to the hospital." "Okay, coming," I squealed and accidentally hung up on her.

Eddie and I were like two spiraling tornadoes, running around our home, leaving a mess in our dizzying path. Our neat, unflustered, peaceful home looked like the final scene in a Jason Bourne movie. When we finally assessed that enough blue junk had been loaded into the car, we jumped in, slammed the doors sweating, and backed full speed out of our driveway. We were on our way to get our little man.

• • •

I will never forget the walk into the hospital. With my pounding heart, clammy hands, weak voice, and flushed face, we made our way inside. We checked in with the nurses' station as a precaution before entering the room marked with the last name of our birth mother. The nurse behind the counter smiled and said, "We have been waiting for you. Go on in." With a glance of affirmation to each other, Eddie and I entered the room bearing flowers and candy in an effort to make our meeting more successful.

I will not forget the moment my eyes met her eyes. There was intoxicating emotion as I walked to her bedside to hug her. Her small frame willingly hugged my neck as she assured us she was glad we were there. Chatter filled the small room as we talked about the delivery and health of her son—our son. Then it happened. The door opened and in rolled a small translucent hospital bassinet with our most precious cargo. I thought my heart would stop as the nurse softly yet happily said, "He is beautiful." His birth mother immediately directed me and said, "Pick him up." And maybe for the first time in my life, I was shy and said, "I want to be respectful of your emotions." She quickly replied, "But Autumn, he is yours." And he was ours. He was my son created to be a Miles.

• • •

Exactly forty-eight hours after the birth of Moses, we reentered the same hospital room with him securely fastened in his small black car seat ready to head to Dallas. The room felt different. There was no chatter of the birth or delivery, but a darling birth mother sitting upright in an uncomfortable hospital chair, a mobile tray rolled up against her lap. The air seemed warm in the room, maybe even stale. The lights were almost completely off, and I struggled to make out what sat in front of her.

When the representative from our agency turned on the lights, I saw plainly the stacked papers on the tray and a pen in our birth mother's hand. As our representative directed and explained, she signed the documents. Some papers she paused on and others she signed immediately until there was only one left. It was the most important one yet. The agency representative stopped and explained something like this: "Do you understand by signing this paper, you are terminating and relinquishing your parental rights as a mother to this child? This action is irrevocable." Everything in the room seemed to pause as she answered yes and with a shaky hand penned her signature to relinquish her parental rights.

Tears filled my eyes as I watched the emotional pain in hers. My knees weakened for a moment. We'd fallen completely in love with our little Moses in the last forty-eight hours. Every time I picked him up, he calmed. Every time his eyes opened, he saw us and slowly began to respond. We wept in the waiting room with anxiety and love all at the same time. He wasn't born to us but born for us. He was the child for whom we'd prayed and waited.

The spiritual adoption process made so much sense all of a sudden. Leaving Moses during those forty-eight hours in the hospital each night had been torture. But finally, even though the ink was still wet, the papers had been signed and he was ours. As much as his birth mother loved him, circumstances wouldn't allow her to keep Moses, so she offered her life for his. In an effort to save his life, she sacrificed her own in a way others perhaps wouldn't call a sacrifice. For a time, she willingly and sacrificially silenced her feelings, emotions, preferences, and happiness. She surrendered to the loss of her love, gratification, and even her physical touch in order to give her son the opportunity for a better life she couldn't provide. Her sacrifice gave Moses's life hope.

It was raw. It was an example of the gospel in real time. God offered his Son for us because we were worth the very sacrifice of his Son to him. God restrained himself in silence while his Son was on the cross in order for us to have salvation. He sacrificed his innate preference and emotions for us to have hope of a better life. He "so loved the world, that He gave His only begotten Son" (John 3:16).

"OUR LIFE FOR YOURS"

Sacrifice is defined as the destruction or surrender of something for the sake of something else. It is something given up or lost.[12] Whereas risk, which we talked about earlier in the book, is a *chance* of loss, sacrifice is a clear cut, undeniable, sure loss. It is a strong theme in the story of Rahab the harlot, most visible in an oath made between her and the spies.

Joshua 2:14 reads, "So the men said to her, 'Our life for yours if you do not tell this business of ours; and it shall come about when the LORD gives us the land that we will deal kindly and faithfully with you.'" The sacrifice in this pledge went both ways, requiring the spies and Rahab to sacrifice if it was going to work. Both parties had something to lose. I want to focus on the statement, "Our life for yours."

We have already talked about Rahab's risk, but I want to put a spotlight on the spies' sacrifice. Imagine being in their shoes while they lay still under drying stalks of flax. They witnessed Rahab's sacrifice, at least audibly, that is. They would have heard the intimidating knocks of the king's men on her door. I wonder if they held their breath when the threat of death fell from the officials' lips. They would have heard the guards' footsteps when they paraded around her home searching for them. When the men questioned her about the spies' whereabouts, she answered them confidently and clearly. They would have heard her response.

I cannot help but imagine what emotions came over the spies as they took an oath not to just risk their lives for her, but also to give their lives for hers. I don't know what made them decide to initially enter Rahab's house. I don't know if God directed them there. I don't know if they'd done their advance research, spying out the city walls, deciding the location of her home and its ever-revolving door would make them less susceptible to being noticed. But either way, they chose Rahab's house.

The reputation Rahab earned throughout her career, if ever held in judgment, was canceled as far as it concerned these men. They knew no ghetto prostitute who devalued herself after every trick. What they saw was greatness and courage. And they held themselves responsible for keeping her and her entire family safe. That is sacrifice. Rahab and the spies gave their lives for each other.

THE DISSERVICE
OF SELFIE-SERVICE

The type of sacrifice demonstrated by Rahab and the Israelite spies is hard to find these days. It's not promoted as heroic and honorable as it once was. Rather than self-sacrifice, we find a bunch of self-absorption and self-preservation in today's society, fueled by individualism, independence, and social media. Ego dominates as we look to serve ourselves. And the practice of sacrifice is sacrificed.

How about the "selfie" world we live in? Do you spend more than two minutes posing for a picture to post on social media? Do you edit and filter the mess out of it until the picture doesn't even look like you? We are instinctively after a great selfie because the number of likes makes us feel better about ourselves. The compliments stroke our starved egos. The people we share a photo with give us bonus status points. We allow our significance to hinge on others' mindless scrolling and tapping of a flat pixel screen. But if we're honest, we feel dissatisfied with our selfie world because the likes and accolades fall flat too. The confidence boost doesn't last. It wasn't meant to when the Savior died for you.

We make light of the "selfie game" as only a game until it becomes a lifestyle. Focus on self becomes an emotional vortex of discontentment, depression, danger, and even death. Seventy-three "selfie deaths" occurred in the first eight months of 2016 alone.[13] Ego dominates the life that caters to self and subtly destroys it. Obsessing over a positive perception of self on social media feeds the thought processes that are antithetical to selflessness and sacrifice. Self-living is one of the biggest disservices in your life.

• • •

The disservice of self-service rears its head in the form of self-help too. When I was growing up and bombarded with those initially crippling teen issues, I cannot count how many times someone would offer ways of help that centered entirely *around* myself. Some would say, "You need to believe in yourself." They followed the tender rebuke with advice on how to grow in my self-worth or achieve high self-esteem.

Terms like *self-esteem* and *self-confidence* are engrained into our youth as if this were the answer to our innermost problem. We encourage and challenge one another with the phrase "believe in yourself." The concept is arguably well intended, but much about it falls deceptively short. So much focus on "self" has caused a huge problem. It spreads the lie that you can save yourself with enough effort, gumption, and positive self-talk. And Christians have bought it. They've swallowed this lie. Striving to find some inner power in themselves, they fall short.

This cycle has a vicious, unquenchable appetite leading to a dangerous downward spiral if not broken. What we are really seeking can never be found in ourselves because it was never meant to be. What we are seeking can only be found in our Savior. Our culture preaches a cheapened message of "self" rather than Savior. It's a disservice to you. "Self" was never created to do what the Savior will do for you.

A few years ago, a team member asked to have a meeting with me. She was a precious, strong woman, even if she always seemed to be on the quieter side of the personalities on our team, but she was so reliable and loyal. I loved having her on the team. When I met with her, she had one question: "Where does all your confidence come from?" She continued, "You are so self-confident, and I don't think I could ever be like that." A huge smile came over my face. Not because I was laughing at her, but I knew my inner me. I knew I did things scared, and when I took a huge step of faith, I would often cry out to God for hours before taking it to the team. I knew what my inner self was like. She clearly saw confidence where I knew there was weakness. I answered, "Solely from the Lord." I had learned when he asked something of me, there was a reason. I move forward based on that alone, not my self-confidence. I won't put confidence in myself because I know I will fail me. I would much rather put it in the Lord who has never failed me. She had an "aha" moment, and I was glad to be out from under the assumption that my strength came from myself.

When we stop the madness of focusing on ourselves, we shift focus to the Lord. Our greatest service to ourselves actually comes when we die to self. Matthew 10:39 says that whoever "has lost his life for My sake will find it."

YOUR LIFE FOR MY LIFE

Our culture has adopted a mentality opposite of the self-sacrifice we see in Rahab and the spies. Culture is in it for the personal win and gain. Our mode of operation is "your life for mine," or even "your life for my agenda." We live it proudly.

It's hard to admit we act like this, but maybe familiarity strikes when you think about it this way: "Your time for my purposes," "Your heart manipulated to my advantage," "Your exhaustion and overextension for my rest and quiet," "Your pity for my business or financial gain," or "Your gifts and talents for my goals." It hits closer to home now, doesn't it?

I'm surprised we don't make T-shirts to display our selfishness. I wish I could say this nicer, but honestly, this mentality makes me sick. (Insert puking face emoji.) Can I be this real? Here's the deal. In an effort to further ourselves, we sacrifice others. It's that black and white.

Self-service takes from others. It combusts, spewing out everywhere, leaving little untouched. The stories in the headlines of the news haunt us as we continually hear of groups or individuals willing to do whatever necessary for their own comfort, social status, opinion, or cause. James 3:16 leaves no question about the loss incurred by selfishness: "For where jealousy and selfish ambition exist, there is disorder and every evil thing."

We see the concept played out perfectly within the marriage context. If one spouse continuously elevates his or her desires and preferences, it will be to the detriment of the other's security, health, and stability. For example, when one spouse goes outside the marriage and has an affair—even an emotional affair with someone at work—self-service reigns. It's a "your life for my life" mentality. This is not only true with adultery, but within other avenues of the marriage like parenting, cleaning, or working. Our culture feeds a mind-set that elevates whatever I want as more important than what you want. This egocentric behavior kills marriages every single day.

The same way of thinking rears its ugly head in social issues like abortion. The one carrying the child chooses to abort based on her desires and perceived needs. The child is sacrificed rather than released for adoption or parenting. It's a heavy, controversial, serious case of "your life for mine." It's a trap, because most who have had an abortion struggle daily with guilt and regret. They didn't really take into account the nearly crippling weight of the memory of the act that will follow them the rest of their life. Let me interject here for those who have aborted a child. God loves you desperately and can forgive you. He doesn't want you to carry the regret one second longer. His sacrifice for you covered that abortion.

Sweet reader, this mentality has even crept into our churches and Christian circles. We see leadership getting slammed if they are too direct about teaching the Word of God. Far below the priority of the gospel being preached and lives being changed, things like the volume of the music on a Sunday morning or the color of the auditorium carpet are complained about on a regular basis. Our preferences and likes are not wrong in and of themselves, but if the way the pastor dresses or if the number of people who greet you dictate your involvement at church, there is a huge problem. Frankly, and I say this in love, we need to stop the entitlement mentality within the church. I am convinced God did not design the church to act this way. It's sinful. The church of Acts didn't have carpet to complain about because they were too busy sharing food and houses. They didn't have a huge "self" problem because they were trying to not be killed for their faith. The church of Acts would be appalled if they knew some of peoples' greatest concerns instead of the gospel of Jesus Christ.

We who bear the name Christian should have better things to think about, for crying out loud! But "better" comes by dying to ourselves. Serving others will come as a natural result of this heart posture: "For to me, to live is Christ and to die is gain" (Philippians 1:21). Let's get over ourselves. When we get our eyes off of self, we are more open to sacrifice. Self is an amazing thing when it is given, a powerful force against the forces of evil.

Does this convict you? It should! It did me. We need to call a bluff on the "your life for my life" mentality and consider the embarrassingly rare practice of sacrifice as the better way. There's something greater in the sacrificial example of Christ. His arms weren't outstretched to get the best selfie view or to take for himself. The Savior's arms were outstretched in order to give up everything through death on a cross while you were at your worst.

WE ARE NOT OUR OWN

Just a day after we were matched with Moses, I received a call from a different adoption contact. She said, "We know you were just matched with a boy yesterday, but a woman has chosen you to parent her daughter if you would be willing to parent her." Cut to us on the other side of the line, silent and shocked, which never happens for me! So just nine weeks after adopting our son, my husband and I brought home our daughter.

Yes, it was *a lot*. But God told us to adopt. Rahab and Jesus challenged my thought processes around self. So when we were presented with the privilege of two children, we immediately said yes. This verse wouldn't get out of my head: "Or do you not know . . . that you are not your own? For you have been bought with a price: therefore glorify God in your body" (1 Corinthians 6:19–20). Moses and Haven Miles have changed our lives in a way our comfort or self-preferences couldn't have. I cannot imagine if we'd been unwilling to adopt either of them.

* * *

Imagine for a moment if the spies were unwilling to sacrifice their lives on behalf of Rahab. What if they were so consumed with following their dreams to conquer Jericho and be heroes that they gave no genuine time of day to Rahab? What if they were so obsessed with their own safety and agenda in the pending battle that they were unwilling to risk the rescue of Rahab and her family? What if they didn't want to be judged by their fellow Israelites for such a gracious arrangement with a harlot, so they told her they'd *try* to help but then decided they didn't want to be inconvenienced by it? We can only imagine the consequences of how a self-absorbed "your life for my life" mentality would have played out. Praise God the spies were willing to sacrifice to be obedient to the call of God.

What does Scripture tell us a life of sacrifice looks like? It can look like a lot of things. John 15:13 says, "Greater love has no one than this, that one lay down his life for his friends." So maybe it's picking up your friends' lunch bill or sacrificing your time to help them with a move. Bring them dinner when they have a bad day even if you are busy. Maybe you could watch their kids. First Corinthians 13:5 says love "does not seek its own." So maybe a life of sacrifice looks like letting your husband pick the movie or not defending yourself to someone even if you think you're right. Romans 12:10 says to "give preference to one another in honor."

So maybe a life of sacrifice is giving your employee a shout-out or honoring your friend with your words. Maybe it's walking up to your pastor after church and telling him how much you love him.

You will not be sold short in pouring out your life. Are you with me today? Evaluate your heart. Our crazy world needs your sacrifice. Remember Rahab's life. You can be Rahab. Choose to be.

THE GREATEST SACRIFICE

Jesus willingly endured the ultimate sacrifice in a humiliating, painful death on a cross for you and me. Even unbelievers respect him because of how he as a suffering servant gave his life for ours. His entire life was lived out obediently to prepare for his own sacrifice. He knew his purpose was to offer his life so we could have life.

> He was despised and forsaken of men, a man of sorrows and acquainted with grief; and like one from whom men hide their face He was despised, and we did not esteem Him. Surely our griefs He Himself bore, and our sorrows He carried; yet we ourselves esteemed Him stricken, smitten of God and afflicted. But He was pierced through for our transgressions, He was crushed of our iniquities; the chastening for our well-being fell upon Him, and by His scourging we are healed. (Isaiah 53:3–5)

What compels us to live outside of the exploitative "your life for my life" mentality? What draws us to serve others before ourselves?

The example of Christ, our relationship with him, and the truth around a life of sacrifice will be the only things to drive us in a lasting, motivating manner. I think Scripture speaks for itself on this.

If "God is love" (1 John 4:8) and his "love . . . has been poured out within our hearts" (Romans 5:5), "we love, because He first loved us" (1 John 4:19). A life of selflessness is patient, kind, and not jealous. "[It] does not brag and is not arrogant, does not act unbecomingly; it does not seek its own . . . but rejoices with the truth; bears all things, believes all things, hopes all things, endures all things" (1 Corinthians 13:4–7). We are called to "treat others the same way [we] want them to treat [us]" (Luke 6:31). Going against all ego-driven behavior, we are to "do nothing from selfishness or empty conceit, but with humility of mind regard one another as more important than [ourselves]" (Philippians 2:3).

It is a *command* to love your neighbor as yourself. If "Christ Jesus, who, although He existed in the form of God, did not regard equality with God a thing to be grasped, but emptied Himself . . . by becoming obedient to . . . death on a cross" (Philippians 2:5–8), then we, too, must deny ourselves. We must die to our instincts of "me first" and serve one another.

We should be known as Christians for our love and sacrificial service to those we engage with on a daily basis. If we don't have such a reputation, frankly, it's our fault for allowing selfishness to creep into our hearts rather than following the example of Jesus Christ. We must be known for what Christ was known for—his sacrifice for us. Let the world see us sacrificing our desires, securities, preferences, and attitudes for them. Rahab did it. The spies did it. Moses's birth mom did it. Your turn!

Chapter Eight

- - -

I AM GOD'S
INSIDE MAN

I spoke several years ago at an amazing church in North Carolina. I prepared diligently like I always do for the three speaking sessions I was asked to lead. The Word of God consumed me as I went into my time at this church. I could feel God doing something special and could not wait. I just didn't realize the incredible thing he was doing included me.

Friday night I poured my heart out to the audience of ladies. I shared my story of divorce, abuse, and heartache. When I finished, a long line of ladies waited for me to pray with them and give them words of encouragement. Long into the night, I prayed and encouraged each one. And then, finally, there was one individual remaining. One lady in particular waited patiently to speak to me. As I wrapped up my second-to-last conversation, she stood up slowly. I walked toward her and smiled, apologized, and thanked her for waiting. She gave me a half smile and said, "I would have waited longer." I breathed a sigh of relief, thankful for her grace.

She looked at me square in the eyes and whispered, "My husband beats me, and I don't know what to do." I moved to position my ear in a place where I could hear her more clearly. She then looked from side to side to make sure no one could hear and repeated the line. I paused to process it and prayed silently before I answered this precious middle-aged woman. She continued, "I've been married to him for more than twenty-five years, and I don't know how to get out. What do I do?"

My heart broke for this woman as it does every time this scenario plays out at a speaking engagement. She began to cry. She was broken. I began to cry with her, feeling the exact pain she was living. I knew the bondage and pain. I knew the brainwashing. I knew the fear all too well. I once carried the questions and suffocating despair. I knew the danger and I wept with her.

As we cried and hugged for several minutes, I knew the level of understanding I brought to her couldn't have been offered by just anyone. She'd waited to talk to me because she needed someone to say "me too." She needed someone to identify with and offer her hope. I *got* her. Victims of domestic violence have a sisterhood. We are a group of people who have been battered by those who see us as nothing more than a ploy in their scheme for power.

We talked and developed a plan for her to break free from her abuser. She was scared but confident that she needed to get away from him. I suspect my tears of understanding ministered to her probably more than anything I said. As we parted ways, we gave each other one of those looks. You know the kind. It can only be described as a look sisters give one another when they are in agreement and have a mutual understanding.

I wept all the way back to the hotel. This woman's situation alone was enough to make me weep, but the tears fell for a different reason. My divorce was long over. I'd participated in many speaking engagements since then, sharing my testimony in nearly every one. I'd shared tears with a staggering number of domestic violence victims, but for some reason, this one struck me differently.

You see, for years I struggled with being an outsider of the church. My church kicked me out because of my divorce, so my feelings weren't a big surprise. I was ousted from the very place I desperately needed help. These isolating beliefs impacted every area of my ministry. Sometimes, in preparation of telling my story, I would consider the audience first and the judgment I would potentially face. My preconceived ideas about my audience influenced my security, vulnerability, and storytelling. Draining thoughts plagued me. Perhaps I didn't belong in ministry and should never try to give anyone advice because of my past. I was an unfit outsider, wasn't I?

But on that night in North Carolina, something broke off of me and things shifted. God gave me incredible clarity and insight to my own life. For too long, I believed I was an outsider restricted to the sidelines while the really righteous people did ministry. I didn't realize it was *because* of what I went through that I knew God in a special way and could minister on a deeper level. Up until then, I always looked at my abuse and divorce as something I wished I could forget. Not one time did I view it as a way I was equipped to minster more effectively, especially to those who went through something as equally devastating.

I realized for the first time how God's allowance of those awful circumstances meant I understood what most don't. He took me as a woman on the inside of domestic violence and as someone rejected by the church and brought purpose from my places of pain. I was able to successfully minister to those who were still in their own pain.

Couldn't God bring purpose from the most painful places?

Couldn't he call someone to be his inside man? Couldn't he have someone on the inside of those issues bring his hope? Couldn't the understanding and healing he brought me set me up to minister to others?

My entire thinking about what I went through was changed. Though the season had been one filled with unimaginable pain, I began to thank God for what he did for me in it. It became a weapon, fueling the fire of my faith. If God could bring me through complete devastation, he could do the same for others. I was God's inside man. I saw domestic violence on the inside. I saw church rejection from the inside. That night I realized I was chosen to minister to these women not as an outsider, but as an insider.

Sin and pending battles once kept Rahab trapped on the inside of Jericho's walls. But God did not intend for her to remain there. She would be God's inside man to bring down the city walls. Similarly, yours truly became God's inside man as a divorced, abused, outcast woman. I was on the inside and was called to bring down "Jericho walls" of rejection, bondage, and devastation.

INSIDE JERICHO

Let's look at the story of Rahab again. Joshua 6:1 says, "Now Jericho was tightly shut because of the sons of Israel; no one went out and no one came in." There was no opportunity for anyone to merely waltz into Jericho. The inhabitants of the city were aware of the threat of Israel and no doubt knew Israel was coming after them. God's people were ready to assume all the Lord promised them.

Because of the amount of security offered by Jericho's walls, there was divine setup in someone being positioned on the inside of them. God invited someone on the inside to step up to the plate. He invited someone immersed in pagan society to help tear down walls. And he chose Rahab. She was his inside man. Jericho's walls were only as strong as a lying, outcast prostitute's faith in an able God.

• • •

God positions us strategically. If you have ever felt like an outsider, it is a ploy of Satan. Acts 17:26 tells us God determined the appointed times and the very boundaries of man's habitations. You are not where you are by chance.

In our society, there are many "Jerichos." A Jericho is any area shut down to God. It's a place where he is not welcomed. It is any area of bondage. You know the Jerichos—porn, sex trafficking, media, the entertainment industry, domestic violence, sexual harassment, divorce, abortion . . . the list goes on. But God can take care of any wall; he can even position a Rahab on the inside to help bring it down. Maybe God has chosen you to be his "inside man."

God positions us both physically and naturally on the inside of a Jericho. Physically, I'm speaking about things like where you live and what you have been through. In terms of natural positioning, I'm talking about things like your personality and your natural giftedness. These qualities may be important to being God's inside man. We may hate our positioning sometimes, but it is a vital aspect in the way God wants to work with us. Because of this, we need to learn to be content in our positioning. God knows where you are and will raise you up when the timing is right.

Let's dig in—there is so much to chat about. Specifically, I want to highlight my experiences of domestic violence, divorce, and rejection by the church. Not everyone understands these things, but I do because I went through them. What is your thing? What have you uniquely encountered? Which of your experiences do only some understand? It's those things for which I would deem you as God's inside man.

CITY WALLS

Rahab's house was built on the city wall according to Joshua 2:15: "Then she let them down by a rope through the window, for her house was on the city wall, so that she was living on the wall." This is a vital part of Rahab's physical positioning. The size of Jericho is said to have been between six to nine acres. The population of the city and those who took shelter there would have been around a couple of thousand people.[14] Archeological exploration at the site of Jericho suggests the city probably enjoyed a double wall structure, with houses of particularly poorer individuals built between the inner and the outer wall.[15] It is believed that Rahab lived on either the northeast or southeast side of the wall.[16] The spies exited by a rope she let down from her window, so her house was most certainly located between the inner wall and the outer wall with the window accessible to the outside wall of Jericho.

The contextual information helps us understand why no one wanted to live on the outer wall. It was the most dangerous position in the city and home to the poorest. If the city were to be attacked, the people living on the outer wall would have been the first to die. There was no barrier between them and the enemy.

Rahab lived in the ghetto. Her physical position placed her on the outside of any high society social status. She was most definitely removed from any sort of wealth. If her house was around today, I picture it topped with barbed wire. I imagine the sound of gunshots and sirens filling the night. Those with means lived in a much more secure area. It's likely her family didn't have much either; if they did, no doubt they would have moved to a safer neighborhood.

The outer wall of her physical position quite literally enforced and confirmed her position as an outsider of society. I bet she dreamed of a day free from those cold, ugly walls where her circumstances would be different. No doubt she imagined a day where she could live in the swanky part of Jericho. You know, like the part with the grade A school districts, where kids wore uniforms to school and where people could walk the streets at night. In her daydreams, she may have had a Louis Vuitton bag and a killer yoga instructor. I'm sure she imagined what it would be like to live the Real Housewives lifestyle, especially when it came to not having to sell her body simply to make ends meet.

PHYSICAL POSITIONING

I know many reading this have felt like an outsider their entire lives. You may think things like, *I've always wanted to get out of this town or state or area.* You've dreamed of a day when you could move elsewhere. Maybe you live in the ghetto or in an area placing you on the outs of any sort of inner, cool circle in your community.

I want to challenge you to view things differently. Your position, experiences, and the way you were made are not without point. Perhaps they are the very means by which you will participate in the miraculous. Do you realize God wants you to seek him exactly where you are? Do you realize you were made to help break down Jericho walls?

You are positioned strategically like Rahab. If Rahab had known she would be the only one rescued from the walls of Jericho, I'm sure she would have thought differently about living in the ghetto. Living in the ghetto is sure better than being slaughtered with the entire city. She was positioned to be God's inside man. And so are you, exactly where you are.

You have to decide to join God's story in this way, of course. If you don't surrender what you have been through and seek God in it, your story won't be context for breaking through the walls of Jericho.

What has made you feel like you are on the outside? Feelings of exclusion, isolation, and displacement are a mind game Satan uses to make sure you stay there. He knows if you allow God to shine his light on your Jericho, God will win in your story. You must decide to believe God *wants* you and that he wants to work through you. You must agree that God *can* work through you. You must believe that God wants to reveal who he is to you in the midst of your story. No matter what walls have made you feel like an outsider, they are only as strong as your faith. Your faith is in the One who brings you "out of darkness and the shadow of death . . . [where] he shatters the doors of bronze and cuts in two the bars of iron" (Psalm 107:14, 16 ESV).

For what reason is God asking you to be his inside man? Whatever it is, you must see your physical position as context for a divine encounter. God designed you to break down walls with his help. It's his power and specialty, but your faith enables you to be a part of the miracles.

Who could minister to someone who grew up in poverty like someone who has grown up in poverty? Who could minister to a single mom more effectively than a single mom who has successfully raised her kids? Who could minister to a woman who went through an abortion more compassionately than a woman who had one and later experienced God's freedom? Who could minister to a spouse whose head is reeling from an affair more honestly than someone who has been there and found hope? Who could minister better to someone who has been in prison than someone who has come out of prison and is thriving and rehabilitated?

Regardless of what landed you in a certain spot, it is not too far removed from the reach of God. It's often those areas of vulnerability or weakness we think can't be used for good. Yet God has his eye on them and fully intends them to be part of our calling. The part of our life we want to go away or wish had never happened is the exact experience through which we can experience God in a way we never thought possible. And it's where our most incredible purposes can take place.

Do I want to be vulnerable and admit I was once suicidal and plagued with horrific anxiety because of my first marriage, so much so I believed God was going to kill me? No! But he has worked with my willingness to share about my positioning for years. The more vulnerable and honest I am about my need for the Lord to renew my mind, the more God seems to give me favor to continue to reach people. Real people reach people with real needs. Your positioning is part of the purposes of a redemptive, powerful God who wants to reach Jericho walls, both your own and others'.

NATURAL POSITIONING

While we have a physical position in which God strategically places us, we also have a natural position—our individuality, our personalities, who God designed us to be—that allows us to participate with him. Let's look first at Rahab. Who was she naturally? What was she like? There are some things we can assume about who she was even though Scripture doesn't go into specific details.

For starters, she was shrewd. Probably a Girl Boss. She was quick on her feet and she was smart, probably at least in terms of what we call street smart. She learned to survive in a dangerous place and applied that same quick-on-her-feet quality when the spies ended up at her door. We can also surmise she was courageous. Her bold answer to the king's officials was a moment of raw audaciousness. Lastly, she seemed loyal. Once she heard about the Lord and believed, she served him when the opportunity presented itself. Her bent toward loyalty was apparent, too, when she sought the well-being of her family and not just herself.

Each of these instinctive, natural qualities about Rahab were her natural positioning. It is the same for us. Our natural disposition is one of God's greatest resources.

•••

What do you do naturally? How are you wired? What comes intuitively to you? Our natural positioning involves those things innate and instinctive to who we are.

I know I am an extreme extrovert. My extroversion leaves nothing untouched. For instance, I love people and I gain tons of strength by being around them even though I tire myself out eventually. I have a really loud laugh I don't hold back. I cry at almost anything regarding the Lord. I have strong points of view. I am fiercely loyal. I love very hard, which has sometimes led to me being hurt badly. I'm sociable and want to be best friends with everyone. I love when people succeed in their purpose. I am passionate about everything, which can sometimes mean I'm considered dramatic. I prefer to call it enthusiastic! Ha! I am dangerously ambitious and action-oriented. Some of the things I have pitched to my team scare them, but as God has driven me, I have led them. Extroverted. That's me. And I am so proud of it.

I am also naturally a very girly girl. Go with me on this one. I love getting my nails done. My nail guy is in his fifties, and he's my buddy. I love getting my hair done. Who doesn't? Sometimes I wear so much jewelry I look like a gypsy. It's okay. I'm at peace with it. I've rarely seen a designer bag I hate. I am naturally drawn to love (and dare I say respect) those things. So women like me are naturally drawn to me. I constantly get asked about my lipstick color. Does it mean I'm shallow? Or that the person who asks me is? No! It is merely a natural expression of love for feminine things.

When I felt freedom to wear hot-pink lipstick, laugh loud, and love Jesus at the same time, I said no to the legalism the world too often imposes on Christians. I said no to viewing myself as an outsider, while identifying myself as one created perfectly in the image of God. I began to walk in whom God naturally created me to be. Being my raw, real self has encouraged countless more people than the sanitized version of me ever could. I was told in a meeting one time, "I've never met anyone like you." Shocked that this executive was so raw in his statement, I replied, "I have learned I am awesome about being me."

God purposes my natural positioning. I can so easily relate to people who are passionate, extroverted, and love hard. My girliness, fierce loyalty, and dangerous ambition do not need to be minimized but viewed as divine setups. I am God's inside man for those qualities.

• • •

Jesus was God's inside man for you. God positioned Jesus physically on earth in order to save the world. The places in which he lived and ministered, among his fellow Jews, were sometimes even places of rejection. His own people viewed him as an outsider. Yet if it weren't for his death on the cross, we would not have access to Christ and the forgiveness of our sin. Grace would not be possible to make us "insiders."

His physical positioning meant he experienced life as fully human yet fully God. He lived in the natural as a boy and man. He understood what it felt like to be tempted in all things (Hebrews 4:15). He knew what it was like to hunger and to thirst (Matthew 4:2; John 19:28). He experienced deep sorrow and grief (Matthew 26:38; Hebrews 5:7). He marveled (Matthew 8:10). We know he also grew in wisdom and stature (Luke 2:52).

God positioned Jesus physically, in the natural, as fully divine and fully human to break down the walls of sin for us. There was no greater "Jericho" than the one he destroyed.

• • •

Rahab the harlot couldn't have known she was created and designed as a natural resource God would work through to save a nation. But God worked through everything about her, even her occupation. There was nothing in her physical or natural positioning that his supernatural power couldn't work with in accomplishing his divine plans.

We, too, are God's literal resources. Everything about who we are positions us for encountering God, knowing him, and participating in what he is doing. Where you live, your social circle, or even what you have been through are all part of your physical positioning. Who are you instinctively? What is your personality? How do you process things, or what are you drawn to? These facets are a beautiful God-designed part of your natural positioning.

Wherever God has positioned you is exactly where he wants you to know him more. It is a place where he offers you the privilege and power of participating with him as his inside man. I challenge you: do not discount what could actually serve as encouragement and a glimpse of the glory of God for another and yourself. You are God's inside man.

Chapter Nine

I AM A CHANGED WORLD

In a quiet whisper she said, "You changed my life." As I hugged her, I knew this could be the last time I talked to her this side of heaven. My tears streaming, I held her face and replied, "Kate, you changed mine." With our precious exchange at an end, I left Philadelphia and made my way back home to my family in Dallas.

Katie Dewan, or Katie De-One-and-Only, joined my team in 2012. She was nineteen when she began working for me. If she were here, she would be sure to remind me I actually interviewed her the year prior and forgot about her. She loved to rub my omission in my face and teased me regularly about what I was missing for an entire year. In my defense, she changed her hair color from dark brown to blonde over the year lapse. It completely changed the way she looked, so, yes, I didn't remember her when I *did* hire her.

She came into our team like a freight train. She was not one with a subtle personality; she was fire. I love colorful personalities, and she quickly became one to watch on our team. She started off working on the social media team, posting on the Blush Network's Facebook and Twitter accounts like a champ but, bless her heart, it was clear her talent was better used in a different area.

Katie loved people and was excellent with them, so we put her on the marketing team. It wasn't long before she transitioned to leader of the marketing team, managing approximately six interns at a time. One of her main objectives was to spread the word about our conferences. Our goal for the Blush Network conferences was to have an audience composed half of churched individuals and the other half completely unchurched. By unchurched, I mean individuals coming from detention centers, homeless shelters, and the like, though the definition can be broader.

I dare say this was the favorite part of Katie's job. After contacting shelters weeks ahead of time, it was not unusual for her to show up at a shelter on conference day with a bus or van to pick up women, only to find out the shelter had forgotten about the event. Katie, who was undeterred and bold, would ask permission to personally invite the residents. She would go through the shelter, convincing residents they needed to attend the conference. She knew if she could get people who seemed to have no hope to attend our conferences, they would hear the gospel of Jesus and almost always surrender to Christ. She took her job and position very seriously.

I often waited with anticipation on conference days for the news of Katie's arrival with the "crew." I knew when they arrived, it was game on! She would walk in with the biggest smile on her face and look at me and say, "I've got some stories to tell you." I loved hearing her say that, because I knew by faith there would be new creations in Christ once the day was finished. Old things were about to be gone and new things were on the way.

At one specific conference, thanks to Katie's persistence, nearly all of our attendees were unchurched individuals. They came from all over and we bussed them in. At one point, my entire team was personally sharing the gospel one on one with these women. Their surrendered hearts represented all sorts of lifestyles, and heaven cheered. I walked by Katie at one point and we high-fived. One high five and a look as if to say, "Can you believe we get to do this?"

• • •

As our ministry grew, it was evident I needed help in Dallas with the demands on my schedule. I needed boots on the ground. I didn't hesitate when Katie's name came up in conversations with our lead team about who would be the best option to join me. When I presented the idea to her, she prayed about it and quickly agreed to make the move and begin working as my personal assistant. My admiration for her became active dependence on her. She was always an encouragement, cheering us on and saying, "We can do it" or "Let's go for it."

She internalized the vision God gave me in 2003 to change the world with the power of God's Word. She lived it. She breathed it. She bled "Blush." Not only did she embody the vision of a bold, passionate believer, she educated me on spray tans, eyelash extensions, the unspoken rules and etiquette of Instagram, and everything in between. She was my buddy and my sidekick, and I loved her like I loved one of my own kids. She wasn't perfect, but something about her imperfection was endearing. We loved to joke together, and 97 percent of the time, we were laughing at things only the two of us thought were funny.

On December 26, 2015, the day after Christmas, she passed out cold in my house. This wasn't the first time she had passed out. Despite numerous tests and doctor visits, her medical team couldn't explain the phenomenon. I called 911 and went to the hospital with her. Once again, the doctors gave her a clean bill of health, but

I think both of us knew something wasn't right.

Five months later, my husband and I met with her in our living room, and I looked at her and said, "Katie, I don't know why, but you need to return home to Philadelphia." I couldn't explain what I was feeling. I knew the Spirit of God was speaking to me, but I couldn't give her a reason for my assertion. It was one of those things God prompted me and her to obey without it making sense. Sometimes, he asks you to trust him even when it hurts deeply. Both Katie and I didn't understand, but we were committed to what the Lord was saying. It was a somber, loving, almost confusing exchange. Neither of us had any idea what was going on, but we knew she needed to move back home.

Sometimes God will wreck your plans for his. He sees the future and knows the importance of what he is doing.

• • •

It wasn't two weeks later I received calls at 11:00 p.m. from both Katie and her mom. Katie had been diagnosed with brain cancer, specifically with grade IV glioblastoma. The prognosis wasn't good. She needed a miracle.

Days later I was on a plane to Philadelphia. Surgery was underway to remove one of her three tumors, and I arrived as soon as it was finished. I was welcomed into her recovery room, and shortly thereafter she asked for the room to be cleared to be alone with me. She said some incredibly precious things, but one in particular was seared in my mind: "I have big dreams and want to tell the world about Jesus and everyone around me. You have to tell them for me." My reply to her was simple: "I don't have to tell them anything. You are telling them about faith in Jesus simply by clinging to him right now. Your life is preaching." With words both of us were confident that they came from the Holy Spirit, I continued, "You have always wanted a stage to proclaim God's power, and God has given you a stage. This bed is your stage, so preach."

---•••---

On September 24, 2016, our great God chose to relocate Katie to heaven. She was healed instantly with her transition to heaven. She was full of big dreams and wanted to reach the world with her life. She desperately wanted God to work through her. In a recorded video played at her God-glorifying funeral, she said, "Jesus is everything. When you are facing death, you realize nothing else matters. Jesus is everything. God is everything."

Throughout her short life, Katie didn't realize how much she was changing peoples' lives because she ministered out of an overflow of her own changed life. Thousands of lives have been challenged and altered not because of Katie, but because of what the Lord did through her. Her surrender enabled our great God to move through her to gather lost sheep and have them come home. Her life will continue to have a global impact because she chose to have her life changed by God first. I miss her terribly every day.

---•••---

Lives like Katie's make it hard for me to buy into the mentality preached by the world about how to change the world. I hear all the time from people who have a dream to change the world, but they haven't allowed God to change their world and hearts first. Want to change the world? Want to be a legend? Press pause on executing those grandiose ideas to consider first whether those dreams carried for the world reflect the reality of your life.

In order to change the world, you must first let God change your world. You must let him change your thought process. You must learn his ways and his principles. Changing the world simply cannot happen without the transforming power of God. We hear people say they are changing the world, but are they? Or are they just helping a piece of it? The only One who has the power to change the world is the God who sent his Son, Jesus, to save it. And the only way we can truly transform the world is by surrendering and allowing the power of the gospel of Jesus to profoundly change every part of our world.

Changing the world doesn't come easy. It costs us. It's sacrificial. It's risky from the natural perspective. Change takes work. It's not glamorous, luxurious, or enchanting. It's not easy. But when we take our personally changed world and offer it to the Lord, we won't know all the ways our lives will be used to influence others for the Lord. Katie did not choose to change lives by the vehicle of brain cancer, but she was resolute in her faith in Jesus Christ. She was committed to being a vehicle for God to work through no matter what that meant.

FOR THE LORD YOUR GOD,
HE IS GOD

Rahab depicted the principle of change I'm talking about. She was first changed by her faith in God. This led her to make decisions in alignment with the ways of God, which meant she found herself working with Israelite spies and assisting the nation of Israel. Her proclamation of faith became more than just words.

Joshua 2:11 speaks to Rahab's proclamation of faith: "When we heard it [the acts of God], our hearts melted and no courage remained in any man any longer because of you; for the LORD your God, He is God in heaven above and on earth beneath." As Romans 10:17 says, "Faith comes by hearing, and hearing by the word of God" (NKJV).

Rahab experienced true conversion, and her powerful proclamation of faith brought about her work for the Lord. Her faith worked and was active. If her faith had been inactive, it would have been dead and, ultimately, would have claimed her life indirectly. Because she stepped out and risked for God, she was saved physically too.

We may say we have faith in God, but is it an active faith or a dead faith? James 2:17 says, "Even so faith, if it has no works, is dead, being by itself." I don't want you to get confused with this emphasis on what we do and think our works save us. As Scripture clearly states, faith alone saves (Romans 3:28). We cannot save ourselves by works, striving, or performance. However, genuine faith will bear fruit. It achieves because it is coupled with works. Living a life of working faith is hard but necessary.

- It is the way we come to know Christ. He is the very object of our faith and hope (John 14:6; Romans 10:9–10).
- Without faith it is impossible to please God (Hebrews 11:6).
- We overcome the world by our faith (1 John 5:5).
- Faith is the assurance of things hoped for and confidence that God's promises for us will come to pass (Hebrews 11:1).
- Faith moves mountains (Matthew 17:20).
- Faith heals (Mark 10:52).
- Faith is part of our ministry (1 Timothy 4:12).

James 2:26 says, "For just as the body without the spirit is dead, so also faith without works is dead." Dead faith is powerless faith. You cannot change the world if your faith is dead. If your faith is alive and coupled with works, though, you can change the world, starting with your own.

I see people in both the Christian culture and outside of it wanting big things, filled with dreams to change the world, but they give up when work is required. If your external work is going to be of lasting, extraordinary value, then internal, active faith must precede and direct your steps.

Confusing God's ways with socially acceptable mentalities will leave you with dead faith. I've observed in our Christian culture patterns and lies, subtle and not, that must be challenged if we want to change the world. When you have the living power of Christ within you, you have something to offer the world. Let's explore specific areas where faith necessitates work for life change to happen, in your world first and then others'.

Promise of God without the Wait

We are a culture quick to receive a promise from God, but we begin to hesitate when a waiting period is attached. We will take the promise in faith all day long but, Lord, don't make us wait for it. By definition, a promise is a declaration that something will or will not be done, given, etc.[17] When someone promises you something, it's something understood to take place in the future. This trips up so many people. They want the promise and want the promise executed immediately. God does not necessarily work this way.

Our faith comes into play when we believe God's promises. Our spiritual work comes into play when we must wait *well* for its fulfillment. Second Peter 3:8 offers a healthy reminder about God's timing: "With the Lord one day is like a thousand years, and a thousand years like one day." He is not in a hurry.

Abraham knew well the work of waiting. In Genesis 12:1–3, God made a covenant with Abraham, promising to make of him a great nation, to make his name great, and to bless all the families of the earth through him. Part of the promise meant he and his wife would bear a son who would inherit the covenant. The promise of a son was not fulfilled until an estimated fifteen years later when

Isaac was born.[18] God was faithful to his word, but it did not happen as quickly as Abraham wanted. Change happened first for Abraham before it would impact thousands upon thousands in his family line.

A promise by itself is a privilege. If we take God's promises and claim them as our own, we must not become impatient when they don't happen according to our time frames. God's plans are never carried out on human timetables. We must do the work of the wait in order to receive the promise. By the end of the wait, learning to trust God and seeing his faithfulness will have changed our hearts. The evidence of God's promise in our lives will encourage others. Faith coupled with works, in this case waiting for the promises of God, changes worlds.

Stage without Stewardship

I receive messages all the time from those who have a desire to write books or speak from big stages on behalf of the Lord, but when asked to share at a small group, they decline. Our pride cannot be bigger than our opportunity. So many want a stage or greater influence, but they do not want to do the work of stewardship. Small opportunities that are stewarded well give way to bigger opportunities.

The parable of the talents in Matthew 25:14–26 gives us a great example of the importance of stewardship: A master went away and trusted his servants with a certain amount of talents: one received five, one received two, and another just one. When the servant with five worked and made the master five more talents, the master responded, "Well done, good and faithful slave. You were faithful in a few things, I will put you in charge of many things; enter into the joy of your master" (v. 21). The master responded the same way to the one who received two talents and yielded him two more. The slave who received only one talent, however, hid it in the ground due to fear. It yielded him nothing. He was called "wicked" and "lazy"

(v. 26). Fear, the antithesis of faith, kept the last slave hindered in his work. He changed nothing for his master and made his own life worse. In contrast, the ones who put in the work of stewarding the talents well were blessed.

We may have faith that God is going to give us a big ministry stage, a big fancy job or opportunity, or to increase our spheres of influence, but the work of stewardship must be applied. Also, what if the stage of your life looks different from what you had in mind? We won't become whiney and debilitated because of disappointment if we steward our heart and trust God's purposes, learning to love him more than what we *think* we can do for him.

First Peter 4:10 says, "As each one has received a special gift, employ it in serving one another as good stewards of the manifold grace of God." You want to steward your life well and change the world? Love God and love people right where you are. Your faith is at work when you do so. At the end of the day, stages and influence don't come without proper stewardship. It's one of God's principles.

Revelation without the Study of God's Word

We want the revelation of God without the work it takes to receive it. We must be students of the Word of God in order to get revelation from him. It takes work to know what God's Word says. We are so quick to turn on a podcast of our favorite preacher or biblical speaker to be spiritually fed, but we need to be feeding ourselves daily with the sustenance of God's Word. If we don't, we'll miss out on an encounter with God. We'll also lead ourselves down the wrong path. Second Timothy 4:3 says, "For the time will come when they will not endure sound doctrine; but wanting to have their ears tickled, they will accumulate for themselves teachers in accordance to their own desires."

For years, I have done selfie videos on my Facebook page. I

started them in 2011 when we launched the first ever Blush Network conference. I sat at my kitchen table and shared what was on my heart. Since then, millions of views later, what I have shared has been something out of my own study of God's Word. These videos are unproduced and come straight from my cell phone, but when I get a strong revelation from God's Word, I am compelled to share it.

But I have to do the work to receive it. I spend time learning how to study the Bible and hear God's voice. Revelations don't just show up in my brain one day. Those videos take my faith working.

Your faith for the revelations of God in his Word must be coupled with the work to actually *be* in God's Word. Hebrews 4:12 speaks to the life-changing quality of the Word: "For the word of God is living and active and sharper than any two-edged sword, and piercing as far as the division of soul and spirit . . . and able to judge the thoughts and intentions of the heart." You're changed first by the Word and thoroughly equipped for every good work because of it (2 Timothy 3:16–17). Sounds like a good way to bring change to the world, doesn't it?

Wisdom without the Trial

We want to be wise, but wisdom entails more than we like to accept at times. Trials are one thing God uses to test our faith, teach us, and develop wisdom in us. Our faith must be at work when we face trials.

James 1:2–5 speaks to the value of trials: "Consider it all joy, my brethren, when you encounter various trials, knowing that the testing of your faith produces endurance. And let endurance have its perfect result, so that you may be perfect and complete, lacking in nothing. But if any of you lacks wisdom, let him ask of God, who gives to all generously and without reproach, and it will be given to him." The testing of our faith is purposed to make our faith genuine. Trials no doubt leave us with questions, but we can ask God for wisdom in them. He promises to supply it. And the supernatural wisdom of God far surpasses the wise ways of man.

As I look back on my life, nothing has taught me more about God and his character than watching the Lord work through my trials. No matter the trial, I silence myself and watch how God works it out in my favor, staying focused on him alone. The work on my part involves intentional times of prayer, a kingdom perspective, and obedience. My faith cannot be passive when I face the brunt of a trial.

Too often, society takes a passive approach to trials, or tries to avoid them completely. People numb themselves with fleeting pleasures, busy themselves, or hurry past the hard work of trials . . . all the while missing out on the beauty God can bring forth from difficult situations.

God never tells us to give up. He wants us to grow up in our faith and, in turn, wisdom is produced in us. Stand in active faith and watch what God will do for you. First Peter 5:10 says this about your trial: "After you have suffered for a little while, the God of all grace, who called you to His eternal glory in Christ, will Himself perfect, confirm, strengthen and establish you." A confirmed, strengthened, and established you has a lot to offer the world.

Answered Prayer without Praying

Before you say this one is elementary, pause to consider your prayer life. I have long talked about prayer becoming a dead language. I don't believe it is one, but our lack of discipline, faulty beliefs, and insecurities render us with rehearsed lines and quiet whispers of doubt. What if we instead prayed in a way that was fervent, confident, and sincere? What if we expected God to answer and paused to listen? What if we did the work of spending time in prayer with God?

I coined a phrase years ago: "Gangster Prayer." When you hear of gang members in any sense (go with me here), they are intensely passionate about their cause. They even sacrifice their lives for their cause. Something about such dedication, work, and fervor spoke to me. I realized wimpy, weak prayers didn't exactly yield miraculous results because they were not rooted in faith. My long-shot prayers were problematic because I was focused more on myself and less on the truth of who God is. My prayer life changed when I understood God *wants* us to expect him to come through rather than just expecting him not to answer.

What if I was as passionate about my prayer life as the gangster is about his or her cause? Clearly there are two totally different objectives, but in my mind, I have the One who is powerful enough to move heaven and earth on my behalf. Shouldn't I expect him to do so when my prayers align with his will? First John 5:14–15 is clear: "This is the confidence which we have before Him, that, if we ask anything according to His will, He hears us. And if we know that He hears us in whatever we ask, we know that we have the requests which we have asked from Him." In other words, we get a yes from God when we pray according to his will.

I began to pray as if my life depended on it . . . because it did! I love the story in Luke 18 about the woman who went before the unjust judge so many times with a plea for protection, the unjust judge granted it to her. Her hope was coupled with the work of persistently bringing her requests before the judge. The woman literally threatened to wear out the unjust judge with her repeated request. Jesus responded by asking, "Will not God bring about justice for His elect who cry to Him day and night, and will He delay long over them? I tell you that He will bring about justice for them quickly" (vv. 6–8). If an unjust judge finally granted the woman's request, will not our God hear and answer the prayers of his children so much more? The work of prayer is more than worth it as Jeremiah 29:12–13 describes: "Then you will call upon Me and come and pray to Me, and I will listen to you. You will seek Me and find Me when you search for Me with all your heart."

Breakthrough without the Breakdown

We always want a breakthrough in our situation, but sometimes it will come only when we reach the bottom of ourselves. When we break down, we essentially cease striving in our own ways and surrender to God. We look to God and to his truth that we so desperately need in order to move forward.

If breakthrough means advancing or moving through an obstacle, then at times this will involve letting go of things holding us back. We have to be willing for God to remove the things in our life not bearing fruit. If God takes things away from us, it is done in love. Let me be clear to say I am not speaking about the things taken from us by sin and this fallen world. I am talking about the pruning work of a master gardener who knows what is best for our growth. The Word tells us in John 15:1–6 that every branch that does not bear fruit, he takes away.

There was a season in our ministry when it seemed everything was going amazingly. We were growing or, at least, it seemed so from the outside. We may have been growing numerically, but I sensed something wasn't right. Not long after the Holy Spirit's prompting, God began to take away staff and opportunities. Now at first I was completely freaking out. I begged God to intervene, but I didn't realize he was pruning us and breaking things down for the purpose of something better.

I decided to take my own advice and surrendered my will to the Lord's. As soon as I did, I was at peace, and I waited for God to do what He is so good at—restoration and rebuilding. What followed was one of the most incredible growth spurts we ever experienced as a ministry. Within months, we were so overwhelmed with work we hired more people to keep up with the load. In the breakdown, God gave us a breakthrough of growth in our ministry.

Surrender and the utter dependency upon God so often a part of breakdowns can feel like the most horrible spiritual work. But the beautiful discipline is bound to your faith and creates a heart posture for God to bring breakthrough.

Abundance over Giving

Early on in my and Eddie's marriage, we learned we must tithe. Tithing is the practice of giving 10 percent of your salary to the Lord. We never skipped the opportunity to give and, if we did in the early days, it was because we weren't organized. We learned we couldn't afford *not* to tithe.

Tithing is a supernatural principle and discipline that really doesn't make sense in the practical, but it produces amazing results. It is our faith manifested in action. The Bible says in Malachi that if we test him with our giving, God will pour out a blessing on us so great our storehouses cannot even hold it (3:10). God also says he will rebuke the devourer on our behalf, meaning he will stop the ploys by the enemy to devour our earnings (v. 11). I don't know how, but it works.

There were days I didn't know how we were going to pay our bills, but we wrote our tithe check each month and out of nowhere, things would happen. We would get a check in the mail or someone would bless us. Now, after fourteen years of marriage, we give more than we ever have and literally cannot outgive God. We have even tried to tithe our entire year's salary before and somewhere, somehow God found a way to give it back to us.

In contrast to the biblical practice of giving, our world's message is to get all you can. Have the fancy bags and clothes and drive the nice car. Go take the trip and treat yourself, the world screams.

But less often do messages about giving filtrate our days. Even in churches, only between 10 and 25 percent of a typical congregation tithe (that is, give at least 10 percent of their income to the church).[19]

What you need to understand about your faith at work in the area of giving is that when you give, you engage a God who is the ultimate Giver. He so loved the world, he gave his only Son. He wants nothing more than to give back to you. There were many days Eddie and I gave in faith. It was literally our faith at work believing God would come through, and the more God came through, the more our faith grew. Giving actually became fun to us. Now we give everything away, even our home. We don't even say it's ours. It's clearly God's. He gave it to us and he can use it any time he wants. Because of our mind-set, we have hosted some of the most amazing people and parties at our house. Those who enter know our house as a safe and comfortable place.

You want abundance? You want to be able to bless others and change the world by giving? The ways of God command giving back first to God what is already his and sowing into others. We don't give to *get*, but the rules of sowing and reaping apply. Whatever a man sows, that he will reap.

• • •

I know my words have come as a challenge, but I say them in love. (Insert heart-eyed emoji.) Just as God worked mightily through Rahab and my dear friend Katie, God wants you to know him more through these areas of discipline. He wants to work through you to change the world, but he must change your world first. You must understand and obey the principles he puts forth in his Word. You've got to put forth some work to bring kingdom light to this dark world and advance the gospel in an impactful way. The faith that came to you by hearing (Romans 10:17) will be fully alive and active, not dead and dormant.

We believe, and we respond. I adore you, friend. I simply adore you.

> For if anyone is a hearer of the word and not a doer, he is like a man who looks at his natural face in a mirror; for once he has looked at himself and gone away, he has immediately forgotten what kind of person he was. But one who looks intently at the perfect law, the law of liberty, and abides by it, not having become a forgetful hearer but an effectual doer, this man will be blessed in what he does. (James 1:23–25)

Chapter Ten

I AM ON TIME

L ast summer I was booked to appear on a segment of a Christian TV show. The booking happened to be during my family's annual two-week vacation. While not ideal, my husband and I decided I should proceed. The show would feature a study I'd commissioned with LifeWay Research about domestic violence and the church, so we felt like my being there to represent the work was important. To this day, I believe one of my appointed purposes involves my work on the study.

We left to drive the three hours to our hotel for my appearance early the next morning. I love to travel with my husband. He is the calm to my crazy, and whenever I'm feeling slightly uneasy about anything (or feel like I am going to lose my mind), he can settle me down with one word. The trip went smoothly. We even stopped and ate a long, leisurely, swanky dinner, which is something we don't experience much with four kids.

We arrived at the hotel around 11:30 p.m., late in the evening and a couple of hours later than when we typically go to bed (call us boring—that's okay). I knew my oldest daughter, Grace, would probably be awake and decided to FaceTime her to let her know we'd arrived. She and the rest of our kids were staying with my parents. I was so glad to see her precious face when she picked up my call. "We are here, and I can't wait to see you tomorrow when I'm done," I said. She told me she was praying for me, and we ended the call just minutes later after an "I love you" battle (basically, we compete to see who can say it more and who can get in the last "I love you" before ending the call). I knew 5:00 a.m. was going to come quick.

I walked into the hotel room, where the pillows called my name, and I plopped down, waiting for my husband to enter the room with our luggage so I could get ready for bed. Seconds later, the Holy Spirit of God spoke loudly and urgently to my spirit, "FaceTime Grace back and tell her to show you Moses's face." He seemed to shout the directive to me. Without hesitation, I called Grace back. She answered with an inquisitive, "Hello?" I spoke fast and said, "I know this sounds crazy, but I need you to go into Moses's room and show me his face in the camera." She rebutted with, "He's asleep, Mom. I don't want to wake him." Almost shouting, I repeated the request the Spirit of God mandated to me and asked her to go.

Two days before, while getting my two-year-old son ready for church, I noticed a few hives. With four kids, we have learned hives can be a very mild concern. We usually treat it with Benadryl and call it a day, and this is exactly what we did. He seemed to improve, but he woke up the next day with them again. I immediately called the doctor, and they assured me we were doing exactly what we needed to do. With a few extra pointers from them, I felt safe leaving and going to the TV show. Before we left, Moses complained of his feet hurting. It seemed to hurt him to walk. As an active two-year-old, he pushed through, so our concern was minimized again. Knowing the kids would be staying with my parents and I could check in regularly with them, we were off.

I held my breath as Grace hurried to the bedside of my sleeping boy. She leaned in slowly and shined the camera light from the phone on his sweet face. I allowed my eyes to adjust to the dim light of the bedroom and focused on his eyes once I could see. To my horror, they were completely swollen shut. Trying not to panic, I told her to shine the light on his lips, and when she did, they were at least five times larger than usual. In full-on panic mode, I began to bark orders at my precious daughter. I knew the condition of my son was bleak.

She obediently followed every command and began shaking him to wake him up. He wouldn't. I screamed, "Get Grandma and Papa up. He needs to go to the hospital now!" My mom ran into the room, with my dad following, to assess the situation. Within minutes, my lethargic, swollen baby was halfway to the hospital.

Eddie entered the hotel room with our luggage, clueless as to the events of the last few minutes. In a state of panic, I tried to articulate what had happened in a few sentences. "We have to go back now. Moses is lethargic and swollen. He is on his way to the hospital." Without hesitation, Eddie rolled the suitcases back to the car for us to drive the three hours to my parents' town.

I stayed on FaceTime with my mom as they frantically sped Moses to the emergency room. The camera of the phone remained on his face, and I prayed over his breathing. I knew time was of the essence. The sooner they arrived at the hospital, the sooner he would be administered the medicine needed to stop the swelling.

Only the worst goes through a mom's mind when something like this happens. There is no agony so great as watching one of your children suffer or be in danger. The absolute horror of knowing his throat was most likely swollen was terrifying me. All I could say was, "Jesus. Jesus. Jesus. Jesus." I didn't know much about what was happening in my little man's body, but I knew God could stop time if needed. I knew God could delay the advancement of what was attacking him. I knew God set my TV appearance for this time, knowing I would never make it to the TV show. In his divine providence, if it were any other night, I would have been fast asleep at 11:30 p.m. I would have already checked on Moses for the night hours earlier. I didn't know much, but I knew Who was in charge of Moses's life and Who roused my spirit at the exact moment to save him.

My parents arrived at the emergency room, and without even stopping to check in, Moses was rushed back to a room where several doctors attended to him. There was a flurry of action. No one was messing around; it was clear Moses's life hung in the balance. He was immediately administered medicine intravenously to try reversing the attack on his body.

Eddie and I felt helpless not being in that room when our son needed us the most. We drove as fast as we could and watched things unfold via FaceTime. Thank God for FaceTime. We spoke the name of Jesus over our son, and we knew he could hear us. As soon as he was given all the medicine deemed necessary, three doctors, multiple nurses, my parents, and Eddie and I watched and stood still. We were at the mercy of God and time.

I have never seen doctors stand and watch over a patient so closely. The room was a somber scene as everyone waited. An hour passed with not much improvement. More meds were given. The doctor leaned over and told my mom, "If you didn't bring him in when you did, we would be looking at a much different fate." Hearing those words made my soul tremble over the timing of God. I knew a tracheotomy was prepped if needed, and I called on the name of Jesus even harder.

And then, as he'd called to Lazarus from the grave, "Lazarus, come forth" (John 11:43), it was as if Jesus himself called to Moses. All of a sudden he began to move his hands and arms. Life returned to his previously lethargic little body. God, in his time, saved Moses's life.

———•••———

Once Eddie and I arrived at the hospital, we ran to Moses's room. We found him fast asleep, resting comfortably in a regular room. My mom and dad were clearly shaken from the event and glad to see us. His vitals were stable and his swelling had subsided. He even had drunk two juice boxes before wiping out from the medicine.

Eddie and I bedded down in the hospital room for the night. When the doctor came to check on Moses early the next morning, Moses heard my voice and jumped from the hospital bed into my arms. He clung to me, comforted by my presence. His mommy was there. He clung tightly, much like I'd clung desperately in security and trust to my great God just hours before, begging for my son's life.

God saved his life. His timing was perfect throughout the whole journey. From alerting my spirit to the problem, telling me to FaceTime Grace, and partnering with medicine, God's timing in it all was perfect.

God's impeccable timing, his authority over time, and the way he works with time gives me confidence. I can know my life and all the things God has stored up for me are on time. Who else could have orchestrated with such strategic precision the timing of Moses's rescue? Months later, the Lord told me I was never supposed to do the TV appearance. He only sent me because he knew I wouldn't be awake at 11:30 p.m. otherwise. Get this, God scheduled that TV appearance for me three months earlier knowing he needed me up late that night. My assignment wasn't domestic violence awareness; it was saving my son's life. His timing is perfect. God is precise.

THE PROMISE AND THE DELAY

The timing of God was perfect in Rahab's life as well. Perfect. Like
. . . *perfect!* When her and her family's lives hung in the balance, she
was faced with the decision to trust God for the timing of his rescue,
which is recorded in Joshua: "So the men said to her, 'Our life for
yours if you do not tell this business of ours; and it shall come about
when the LORD gives us the land that we will deal kindly and faithfully with you'" (2:14). She got the promise, but she didn't know
when she would be saved. After the expectant exchange, a number of
events unfolded in the lives of the Israelites.

1. First, the spies stayed in the hills for three days once they left
   Rahab's house to hide while the king's men pursued them
   (Joshua 2:16, 22).
2. After hiding for three days, they traveled back to the Israelite
   camp and crossed the Jordan River (2:23).
3. Upon return, the spies delivered the report to Joshua
   (2:23–24).
4. Joshua then aroused the entire nation, directed them to
   consecrate themselves, and prepared them to cross the
   Jordan River (chapter 3).
5. After crossing the Jordan River, the Israelites held a
   ceremony to commemorate God's faithfulness in bringing
   them safely into the promised land. The twelve memorial
   stones involved in the ceremony signified the importance
   of each of the tribes crossing the river (chapter 4).
6. A circumcision ceremony followed, and all males were
   circumcised. This was a reminder of their covenant
   relationship with God (5:2–9).
7. More time passed when they took time to heal (5:8).
8. They also celebrated the Passover (5:10–12).

9. The entire nation made the final stretch of the journey from Gilgal to Jericho.

10. Finally, there was the famous seven-day march around the walls of Jericho (6:1–21).

I spell out these events to highlight the position Rahab found herself in. The Bible does not tell us she was briefed on anything once the spies slid out her window. A substantial amount of time lapsed from when she was promised safety and the fulfillment of that promise. She was forced to trust that the passing time of each day did not erase the promise. All of these events were crucial for the Israelites and served as preparation for the great task ahead of them. And though they were pivotal to the Israelites and directed by God, it meant Rahab waited longer.

Have you ever thought about your waiting from such a broad perspective? We could be in a holding pattern because God is also at work in others' lives or circumstances. What may be pivotal to them isn't necessarily pivotal to us but still impacts us in a significant way. What seems like God is delaying in your eyes could actually be God working among others to make it happen. Odds are the thing you are waiting for doesn't just include you; there are many facets to it.

Rahab still chose to trust God when she saw no evidence of God working. As the days went by and her family squeezed into her small ghetto apartment, I wonder how often she stared out the window, no doubt watching the scarlet cord swing in the breeze. I imagine that every morning she checked to see if the scarlet cord was secured. I am sure doubt tempted her. But she hung that rope and expected the spies to keep the promise they vowed to her. She did her part, and she expected God to do his. The scarlet cord was proof of her expectation. She was waiting expectantly. She could have easily lost hope as time passed. She could have easily gone to the king and told him of the plans of the spies, bargaining her life for intel. She could have prepped the king of Jericho to be as ready as possible for an attack by Israel. But she didn't. Though her faith was new, it was not weak. She clung to the promise and expected God would see it through. Are you expecting God to move on what he has asked of you? Have you given up hope that God will come through? I ask you to fasten the scarlet cord of faith and watch for God to move on his promise to you. The Bible tells us that God is not a man who lies, so if he said it, you need to expect it from him.

ACTIVE IN THE WAIT

How do you deal with God when you don't see him actively at work in your life? I find waiting, especially for an unspecified amount of time, can break even the most passionate, patient Christian. Be careful not to mistake what you *don't* see for an inactive God.

Satan will tell you things like, "God has forgotten about what he said" or "There's no activity, so you need to go in another direction." Or maybe the whispers are more strategic, like, "Your husband is never going to change" or even "You aren't going to get married at all." All the while, God is at work in what we don't see. How do you know those chides from evil do not come because evil knows God is at work, putting the pieces together for your promise to manifest? Sight can hinder what faith promises. Don't let it.

When you are facing a wait, face it actively and head-on. Waiting should not be faced passively. Your God is not passive, and you are not to be either. You must trust him, listen to him, pray to him, and take courage in him. Believe he is doing what he said he would do.

I actively waited to start my ministry. I had verses from Scripture that I stood on, and every day that I felt like God wasn't listening, I would refer back to my promise from the Bible. While I was waiting, I said yes to every opportunity for ministry I was offered. If

I was asked to speak at a small group, I would say yes. If I was asked to lead an event for my church, I would say yes. If I was offered to counsel a woman, I would say yes. I knew that while I was ultimately waiting for God to open the door to my own ministry, I needed to gain experience and educate myself in the practical ways of ministry. I worked for ten years for other people, watching, asking questions, taking notes on what kind of leader I wanted to be and what kind of ministry I wanted to lead. This is how I actively waited. I wasn't dormant, having a pity party; I was expecting God to do what he was going to do for me but educating myself at the same time.

Lamentations 3:25 says, "The LORD is good to those who wait for Him, to the person who seeks Him."

Waiting is awful. (Insert mad face emoji.) Especially when we see nothing happening. But according to Romans 8:24–25, we hope for what is not seen anyway! One of my favorite chapters in the Bible speaks so eloquently to the faithful activeness of God even when we are worn out: "Do you not know? Have you not heard? The Everlasting God, the LORD, the Creator of the ends of the earth does not become weary or tired. His understanding is inscrutable. He gives strength to the weary, and to him who lacks might He increases power" (Isaiah 40:28–29). In your waiting, he is right there to give you strength and power. Even now, he is aligning your promises with precision. Remember, his timing is precise. Not relaxed, precise.

WATCHING THE WAIT

The week Moses was born, God told me he was going to give us a little boy and we were to name him Moses. I knew when God picked his name, he would one day lead a movement of freedom for something huge. To make sure of it, we made his middle name Ezekiel. I mean, how can a boy named Moses Ezekiel not do something amazing for the Lord.

While I was calling out to the name of Jesus that horrifying night he was sick in the hospital, God reminded me of his secure future. Although things looked bad, God promised me he was going to use Moses in a huge way. Satan was not going to take what God promised. He didn't have that power. He doesn't have that power. He will tell you he does, but it's a lie. On the outside, it looked like God was inactive for a second. In reality, God planned the events to help save Moses's life.

Can you even imagine Rahab's face the day when the view on her horizon changed from inactive to active? Oh, to be a gnat on the wall in her home when she saw the Israelites marching toward Jericho. I know she and her family were freaking out when they saw God had in fact not forgotten about them. Can you imagine the screams that came from her when she went to the window to check the security of the scarlet cord and saw the Israelites marching toward Jericho? Y'all know she was saying things like, "I told you! I knew they would come!"

They weren't rescued yet, of course. As a matter of fact, there was another delay. Joshua 6:2–3 tells us how God planned to defeat Jericho: "The LORD said to Joshua, 'See, I have given Jericho into your hand, with its king and the valiant warriors. You shall march around the city, all the men of war circling the city once. You shall do so for six days.'" Rahab finally saw what she had believed for when the Israelites came to fight Jericho, but all they did was march for six days. Uh-oh. Not quite the plan of attack she'd probably envisioned. I would have gone crazy. And she was probably going crazy too.

I have put myself in this scenario a hundred times. Can you imagine her watching every day as they marched around the city and then left? Do you wonder if she begged God for her promise to come to pass as their boots stomped around the last corner of those stone walls each time, only to watch the Israelites return to camp?

How many questions ran through her mind while she tried to figure out what in the world God was doing? Keep in mind, the Bible does not speak about any communication occurring between her and the spies until after she was rescued. God didn't tell her his blueprint for the defeat of Jericho. He only provided a blueprint to Joshua right beforehand, and even then it seemed a little weird. Certainly it involved more time than what a typical battle looked like. But God fulfills his promises in his way (not yours, cupcake), right on time and at his pace.

THE PACE OF GOD

We must also trust the pace of God when the process seems delayed. Could God have defeated Jericho on the first turn around the city? Absolutely! But he didn't choose to. Instead, he set a slower pace and ordered the Israelites to march around the city for six days.

God planned for the Israelites to defeat Jericho and for Rahab to be rescued, but it all came with a process and a literal pace. Neither Rahab nor the Israelites could get ahead of God. They needed to trust his timing. If Rahab had attempted to rush the promise, she or her household could have been killed. I am sure she was ready for the Israelites to conquer the city, but God wasn't. Nor was he going to bow to her anxiety or expectation when his ways were higher. God isn't intimidated by our urgency. He is driven by his purpose.

I wonder if you see a means to an end for your promise, and yet God is saying, "Not quite yet." Do you feel like you're just watching what is within reach, wondering when the promise will be fulfilled? Has a man entered the picture, and you believe he could be the one whom God has for you? Have you finally met the person who can connect you for your big break? Did you hear there is an opportunity for advancement at your job? There is a time period between when we first believe the words of God and when those things come to fruition. God's timing works in the in-between even when we can't see it. Even when our promise seems imminent and we are ready, it still may not be quite the time yet. God is concerned less about our wait and more about his timing.

Do not rush the process. Submit yourself to the pace of God. In Rahab's situation, there was nothing she could do to rush the pace, but there may be a way for you to rush it. You may try manipulating the man you meet. You may suck up to the person you network with. You may talk negatively about a fellow employee in order to make yourself look better. I say this in love, but these reflect sins of the heart. We cannot allow pride or fear to have a stronger hold on us than our faith in God. There is a pace in place for the plan.

Seek God and align yourself with his pace. You do not want anything God has to offer prematurely. You may think you do, but you don't. If Rahab had interrupted the divine delay to preemptively seek her own freedom, she could have caused Israel to lose their fight. The pace God sets is both for his glory and for you to receive all he has for you. God wanted victory for everyone. He wasn't willing to sacrifice one victory for the other. There was enough good to go around. His plan was on time, set to a beautiful pace.

THE PROMISES FULFILLED

On the seventh day, Israel came once more to the walls of Jericho. Now was the time for Israel's victory and Rahab's rescue. Let me remind you of the waiting experienced by both parties prior to this day. Technically, God promised land to Abraham in Genesis 12 and 15. Jericho was the first city the Israelites were purposed to conquer as part of that promise. The battle of Jericho was an estimated 675 years after the initial promise.[20] Talk about waiting! Joshua and the Israelites waited for days for the spies to return, then more days to prepare for the battle, and even *more* days to fight the battle the way

God told them to. Lastly, we know Rahab waited, too, without any insight to the specific plans of God.

> Then on the seventh day they rose early at the dawning of the day and marched around the city in the same manner seven times; only on that day they marched around the city seven times. At the seventh time, when the priests blew the trumpets, Joshua said to the people, "Shout! For the LORD has given you the city." So the people shouted, and priests blew the trumpets; and when the people heard the sound of the trumpet, the people shouted with a great shout and the wall fell down flat, so that the people went up into the city, every man straight ahead, and they took the city. (Joshua 6:15–16, 20)

Joshua told the two spies to bring Rahab and her family out of Jericho, as they had promised her (Joshua 6:22). The wait was over.

The miracle-working God who kept his promise to the Israelites caused the walls of Jericho to fall. I studied the excavations of Jericho and was stunned when I came upon one finding in particular. Archeologists who have gone back to the site discovered a small portion of the wall still standing on the north side of Jericho. It did not crumble when Jericho's walls fell.[21] Out of the identified northeastern or southeastern residential quarters, it is believed Rahab lived in the northern one. The fulfillment of Rahab's promise came without fail. She waited, trusted in God's unseen work, and submitted herself to God's pace. The promise came at God's precise timing.

HE DOESN'T DELAY

As you consider the things you're waiting on in your life, I want to encourage you to focus less on your waiting and more on God and his strategic, calculated, genius timing. God is not in a hurry. He is not pressured to respond if the timing doesn't seem right to us.

Consider God's perfect timing in the dawn and dusk of every day. What about the timing of the tides of the ocean, each season, or the rotation of the earth on its imaginary axis? We more blindly trust his wisdom in these things because they are so colossal and the science behind them is so rich. As we wait for the sun to rise, we know God is not late in the promise of dawn. As we watch the tide come in, we don't question whether he will forget to ensure it goes back out. Spring, summer, fall, and winter have remained on time since the beginning of time. The world continues spinning at a perfect pace, not too fast or too slow. You blindly trust the timing of God in these things, which our very physical lives depend upon. We need to also blindly trust his timing in the things our personal lives are intimately made of.

When I say "blindly trust," I don't mean we should walk around naively and aimlessly thinking our promises will be fulfilled. I'm not minimizing the fact that trusting the timing is hard. I mean that we put our trust in God, who watches over his Word to perform it (Jeremiah 1:12). Our focus is on his perfect timing and faithfulness, rather than the wait and whatever we think we lack in it. He is the Creator of time and the Sustainer of time, yet he wrapped himself in flesh and experienced time as we know it. He is not unaware of our waiting, but his unfathomable plans are set to a kingdom calendar.

Galatians 4:4 says, "But when the fullness of the time came, God sent forth His Son." He could have sent Christ into the world earlier, but he didn't. In his long-suffering and infinite wisdom, the incarnation of Christ happened when it did for divine reasons. And it was the right moment in human history. "The Lord is not slow about His promises, as some count slowness, but is patient toward you" (2 Peter 3:9).

Waiting isn't hard when we are consumed more on the One who delivers on his word than on the wait. You can trust him. God doesn't delay. His promises unfold at a perfect pace in his perfect time. Let me close with my life verse:

> For the vision is yet for the appointed time; it hastens toward the goal and it will not fail. Though it tarries, wait for it; for it will certainly come, it will not delay. (Habakkuk 2:3)

Chapter Eleven

—— • • • ——

I AM INTEGRITY

I was completely rushed and hustling to get out of Target as fast as I could with my two kids. At this time in my life, my oldest daughter, Grace, was around five years old, and my oldest son was three.

Going to the grocery store with two young kids is a beast of a task, and I hate it. I avoid the grocery store with my kids at all cost for many reasons. Both of them create a duet of wishes and wants that drove me crazy. "Mom, can we get the pudding pops?" "Mom, can we have bright neon-green healthy yogurt?" "Gross," I reply. "No!" Things get interesting when we walk down the paper towel aisle. It's amazing what children see and decide they want. "Mom, can we have the paper towels with the flowers on them?" "Mom, can we have the toilet paper with the blue letters and animals on the package?" Sometimes I just stop to marvel at the ridiculousness of the requests. After I gave what feels like two hundred "nos," the requests from my cute little peanut gallery pipe down. I don't know if they sense the mom tone or if my most intimidating mom stare frightens them. I feel really proud of my mom stare by the way. I've perfected it.

On this particular Target run, when we rounded the corner for the checkout, the illuminated number eleven lane was like the star of David bringing hope and guidance to my very tired soul. I gave a stern mom glare and a final warning to both kids when I said, "Do not touch anything in the checkout aisle. We do not need mini hand sanitizers, Skittles, Ring Pops, *Us Weekly*, Pepsi, Muscle Milk, or tiny bags of tissues. If you touch anything, you will be in trouble." Both kids nodded their heads in agreement as we entered the lane. Frantically, and still in a hurry, I tried to empty the cart while keeping an eye on Grace and Jude to ensure they didn't knock down an end cap of tiny RITZ Crackers. All seemed to have gone smoothly and we darted off to the parking lot to load our car. I was hosting small group at our house later in the evening and needed to get home.

After getting the kids in the car, I started loading the groceries in. I stopped short when I saw the twenty-four-pack of bottled water on the bottom of the cart. Ugh! I knew instantly the checker had not rung it up. I grabbed my receipt to confirm. Yep. We walked out of Target oblivious to the water being unpaid for. Temptation seized me and whispered, "Just load it and go. The checker didn't catch it . . . you are in a hurry . . . you shop here all the time . . . it's not like you're stealing . . . no one will know."

To be honest, it would have been easy to sell my integrity for a twenty-four-pack of bottled water that day. But after I got my life right with God, I committed I would have integrity and do the right thing. Even when no one knew or was looking, I would be upright. Never again did I want to say one thing and do another. I didn't want a life different behind closed doors than it was in public. I wanted my words and actions to be ones God would honor. I knew he was looking.

After I finished loading the groceries in the car, I got my daughter and son back out and headed into Target with my twenty-four-pack of bottled water. I walked straight back to aisle 11, placed the water on the conveyor belt, and said, "I got to my car and realized I didn't pay for the water. So I need to pay for it." The checker looked at me like I was crazy and said, "Wow, I can't believe you came back in to pay for it! That is really admirable. I'm sure most people would have just left." *I do not want to be most people*, I thought. I want to be one person in today's world with integrity.

I drove home smiling. Grace chimed in, "Mom, why did we have to go back in with the water?" Over the next fifteen minutes I was able to tell her what had happened and teach her and Jude about integrity and why it is important. She looked at me, not even fully understanding the deep truth, and said, "Oh, okay! So, when no one is looking, we have to do the right thing?" "Yes, baby," I replied.

— • • • —

I used to be one who completely lacked integrity. I was good with my words at a young age and used them to say one thing but do another. The half-truths were still lies, though, and I forced myself to live a double life in order to maintain the web of deception.

In my marriage to my first husband, I felt like it was my job to lie. I constantly covered for him and myself. I was the antithesis of someone with integrity. When I surrendered to the Lord that faithful night in 2001 at 3:00 a.m., I was incredibly convicted of how I lived in such dichotomy. Lack of integrity ruined my life. I knew I would need to overhaul my life if I wanted my life to look different. And I knew integrity would be pivotal to putting it back together. I would have to be who I said I was and do what I said I was going to do.

I was committed. I fought within myself at times, but I chose truth moving forward. It cost me friends and family members, but in the end I couldn't live a life shackled by the sin of portraying something I wasn't. The mental game had to be overcome.

DO WHAT YOU SAY YOU'LL DO

Integrity is a firm adherence to a code of moral values.[22] Biblically speaking, integrity means moral innocence and uprightness.[23] I know it's an archaic word that is so 1775, but understand our moral principles affect everything about how we live our lives and make decisions. Honor, fairness, sincerity, truthfulness, and trustworthiness overflow from our integrity.

We see a lack of integrity all the time. The pastor involved in an affair. A boss caught embezzling money. The friend who revealed a secret. The list of situations where integrity has left the building in an obvious way is long. But the subtler areas where integrity is lacking are just as rampant. No one thinks twice about a coworker having an emotional affair on her husband or a colleague who padded his resume to get a job. Using someone else's internet or Netflix login information is a widely accepted behavior despite God's command to us that we not steal. And then there's social media. It's not uncommon for us to represent ourselves totally different on social media from how we actually are.

I'm not trying to come down hard on you, friends (insert winking face emoji), but we need to challenge ourselves to be people of integrity and honor. Integrity is not valued like it was in the past, but God's heart about it has not changed. Integrity is the result of a heart surrendered to following God completely, even in the little things. Listed below are benefits of walking in integrity.

- We walk securely if we walk in integrity (Proverbs 10:9).

- We are guided in our integrity (Proverbs 11:3).
- We are protected, and our enemy does not win against us (1 Peter 3:16).
- Our children will be blessed by our integrity (Proverbs 20:7).
- Integrity delights the Lord (Proverbs 12:22).
- It testifies to who God is and reveals his glory (1 Peter 2:12).

We must be people of integrity if we call ourselves God's. Don't take this the wrong way, but if you aren't a person of integrity, don't be telling people you are a Christian. I want people to know I am who I say I am when no one is looking. I practice what I preach and drink my own Kool-Aid. When I give people my word, I follow through. In a world so robbed of stability and hope, I want to be trustworthy.

How do you want to be known? Ultimately, integrity goes back to two things in my mind: doing what we say we are going to do and being who we say we are. This is what we are going to attack in this chapter. I anticipate a healthy dose of conviction for all of us. It already kicked my hiney and, God love you, I pray it does the same for you.

THE ULTIMATE PROMISE KEEPER

If integrity were absent from the story of Rahab, the results would have been disastrous. She and her entire family could have died. Or the spies could have been outed, jeopardizing the victory of Jericho.

Rahab saved the spies' lives, and in return, she asked them to save her life and the lives of her family members. Let's look at the text. "Now therefore, please swear to me by the LORD, since I have dealt kindly with you, that you also will deal kindly with my father's household, and give me a pledge of truth, and spare my father and my mother and my brothers and my sisters, with all who belong to them, and deliver our lives from death" (Joshua 2:12–13).

The spies' response is recorded in Joshua 2:19: "It shall come about that anyone who goes out of the doors of your house into the street, his blood shall be on his own head, and we shall be free; but anyone who is with you in the house, his blood shall be on our head if a hand is laid on him."

The promise was made, but would the spies keep it? Rahab's life rested on the verbal commitment of two strangers. After they were safe in the hill country Rahab sent them to, they were in the clear. Honestly, they could have chosen to do whatever they wanted then. But their integrity ruled, and they made good on their word. "Joshua said to the two men who had spied out the land, 'Go into the harlot's house and bring the woman and all she has out of there, as you have sworn to her.' So the young men who were spies went in and brought out Rahab and her father and her mother and her brothers and all she had; they also brought out all her relatives and placed them outside the camp of Israel" (Joshua 6:22–23).

The integrity of God, Joshua, and the spies saved the lives of Rahab and her family. The spies' word meant something not only to them but also to Joshua and to the Lord. Remember, God actually commanded Israel to dispossess and destroy the inhabitants of the land of Jericho. I'll talk more on this in the next chapter, but the spies' agreement to save Rahab may initially seem like a surprise in light of this. Yet God's heart is to save anyone who turns to him, so the spies' response actually points to God's integrity. He ultimately saw to Rahab's rescue.

The hearts of the spies were surrendered to the Lord, so the outward act of rescue wasn't a forced display of integrity. Our level of integrity is, in essence, a barometer of our walk with God.

Telling the truth and following through on what we say matters. Back in the day, people made verbal contracts because their words carried such drastic weight. When they said they would do some-thing, they did it. People's words were their bond, and it was a huge deal to be a man or woman of your word.

My dad is a man of his word. He had one important rule as a pastor. He told his secretary he always wanted to take calls from my mom and his kids. He told us kids he was always reachable if we needed him, and it was true. No matter what, if I wanted to reach my dad, the secretary would put me right through. One time I called him on a Sunday night, not thinking he would be preaching, and he answered his cell mid sermon! "Is this an emergency?" he asked. I said, "No," and he replied, "I'm preaching a sermon, can I call you back?" It may seem ridiculous, but it made a huge impression on me. No matter what, my dad did what he said he was going to do. To this day, he always takes my phone call unless he is taking his midafternoon catnap.

We laugh at the old-school reality of words alone as binding. The art of verbal contracts has gone. For instance, banks have so many problems with people falling behind on their loans that in order to buy a house, you have to sign an hour's worth of paperwork. I see the problem time and time again in parenting too. The parents promise the children they will do an activity with them, and though they may mean well, they don't follow through in the expected time frame, if at all. Now, no parent is perfect, but breaking your word repeatedly kills a child's trust. Your child will not see you as someone who keeps your word.

What about you? Do you do what you say you are going to do? Ephesians 4:1 tells us to "walk in a manner worthy of the calling with which you have been called." Part of that means our walk should match our talk. I believe when it does not, we forfeit our integrity. We say we will do something and we flat out don't. We say we will do something and delay so much that the original responsibility is negated. Or we over promise and under deliver. People want others to think highly of them, so they promise to offer them whatever circumstances call for but do not deliver in the end. None of these display integrity. Don't promise it if you can't or won't perform it, or if you will delay performing it.

• • •

I believe not doing what we say we are going to do reflects how we view God and his Word. God's Word is the truth on all subjects at all times. It is concrete, inspired, living, and active. God does what he says he is going to do. Always. He fulfills his Word, for he cannot be unfaithful to himself. He has the utmost integrity and is a man of his word. Christ *is* the Word that became flesh, for crying out loud!

If we don't do what we say we are going to do, I'd argue our view of God and his Word is off. We've made it something less than the very breath of God, because the Word of God *will* accomplish what it was set out to do. It would be a travesty to disrespect God's Word just because your word isn't trustworthy. We cannot project others' lack of integrity or even our own onto the incorruptible Word of God. Just because we haven't kept our own word, or someone else hasn't, doesn't mean God isn't going to keep his.

At the end of the day, being doers of the Word is the true, appropriate response to the Word of God. James 1:21–25 speaks to the role of the Word and integrity in our lives:

> [I]n humility receive the word implanted, which is able to save your souls. But prove yourselves doers of the word, and not merely hearers who delude themselves. For if anyone is a hearer of the word and not a doer, he is like a man who looks at his natural face in a mirror; for once he has looked at

himself and gone away, he has immediately forgotten what kind of person he was. But one who looks intently at the perfect law . . . and abides by it, not having become a forgetful hearer but an effectual doer, this man will be blessed in what he does.

Paul, the author of Romans, says hearers only of the Word delude themselves. Self-deception is at play and integrity takes a seat on the bench. He compares it to someone taking a look in the mirror and then forgetting what he or she looked like. Kind of sounds like living a double life, doesn't it? Kind of sounds like saying one thing and doing another, doesn't it?

In Matthew 5:33–37, Jesus speaks to a practice simple to keep when our lives are ones of integrity:

> Again, you have heard that the ancients were told, "YOU SHALL NOT MAKE FALSE VOWS, BUT SHALL FULFILL YOUR VOWS TO THE LORD." But I say to you, make no oath at all, either by heaven, for it is the throne of God, or by earth, for it is the footstool of His feet or by Jerusalem, for it is THE CITY OF THE GREAT KING. Nor shall you make an oath by your head, for you cannot make one hair white or black. But let your statement be, "Yes, yes" or "No, no"; anything beyond these is of evil.

Simply put, our character should speak for itself, making vows basically unnecessary. Our words should be enough because of who we are. When you do make a promise, a simple yes or no void of deceit, flattery, manipulation and the likes is sufficient. You're a keeper of your word. I'm calling you higher. Our world needs it. Our churches need it. Our kids need it. Our spouses need it.

ARE YOU OPERATING
UNDER THE BAN?

I write this section passionately because I once wasn't who I said I was at all. I lived a double life. I professed to be one thing and people believed what I professed. I led people to believe lies. Ugh, I hated typing that.

Even more than keeping our word, our lives should be the same no matter where we are, be it in the presence of our holy God in worship, at our kids' school, or at home with our families. If you are who you say you are, keeping your word becomes more of a natural consequence. It's the private parts of our lives that matter and trip us up the most.

We can say we're in love with our spouse yet be numb on the inside, addicted to porn when our spouse isn't looking. We can say we've got our habits under control and decline a drink in public yet bond excessively with a bottle of wine every night behind closed doors. We can say we've let it go and smile while hatred and unforgiveness take root.

We can't claim to be one thing while we dabble in, consume, own, or say things that we know aren't right. Snacking on sin while professing righteousness is dangerous.

I was inspired by a piece of scriptural real estate along these lines in the story of Rahab. It revolutionized my thinking. In order to live with true integrity, there are things in our lives we must keep ourselves from. Please, my sweet friends, go on this journey with me and answer this question: Are you operating with things that are under the ban?

Joshua 6:17 starts our story: "The city shall be under the ban, it and all that is in it belongs to the LORD; only Rahab the harlot and all who are with her in the house shall live, because she hid the messengers whom we sent." Here, Joshua reminds the Israelites of the promise made between Rahab and the spies. Joshua goes on in verse 18 to say, "But as for you, only keep yourselves from the things under the ban, so that you do not covet them and take some of the things under the ban, and make the camp of Israel accursed and bring trouble on it."

What was under the ban in Jericho? *Everything in the entire city, including the people.* God commanded the absolute destruction of Jericho in Deuteronomy 20:16–17 as his judgment on the Canaanites' sins. Its total destruction would also protect the Israelites from falling into idolatry. The Israelites weren't allowed to keep anything in the entire city for themselves.

When I read this, I was immediately inspired. I continued reading about what happened after the walls of Jericho fell. Israel moved on to fight the next city, which was Ai. But they lost the battle. This probably came as a bit of a shock, since God had just miraculously delivered Jericho into their hands. God revealed the issue to Joshua when he asked the Lord what was going on. An Israelite by the name of Achan took something from Jericho and thus broke God's command. What should have been destroyed he kept for himself. He didn't keep himself from what was deemed impure by God. When he was confronted and confessed, he and his entire family were stoned and burned with fire. God had been clear about what would happen if they didn't keep themselves from things under the ban—it would destroy them. In this case, it destroyed a family and cost Israel in battle.

My mind began to wander to our Christian world today, and I considered the things God has given a no to. Lust, adultery, gossip, lying, and sex before marriage are a short list of things the Lord bans. How about racism? This has been a huge area of talk the last few years. A little race hate here and little joke there and we are operating in something God says no to. God adores everyone and created all "good." He does not discriminate, yet even in the way we joke we participate in racism. Too often we snack on things God has banned, justifying it or, worse, celebrating it in some of our Christian circles. We would never go to the mall and steal a pair of jeans, but we would log on to someone else's Hulu account. We would never subscribe to a porn magazine, but some people's eyes may linger on a nude scene in a movie. We are believers, wearing the name of Jesus, yet snacking on things God banned, living like an Achan.

Let me be clear. You cannot participate privately in things the Lord bans and expect to live an abundant life. God will not bless you living one way publicly and another way privately. Integrity means we are who we say we are in private and public. We cannot expect God's blessings on our lives if we are genuinely seeking after him in certain areas but are still engaging with things the Lord bans.

God didn't ban things from Israel to be mean. He banned because he knew what would ruin them. The withholding was actually a measure of his love and protection.

When I grasped this concept, it radically changed my life. I needed to stop with the secret sins and rid my life of the things destroying me. I didn't want to claim to be a Christian and live like Achan, doing things God says not to do. Nor did I want my private sin to impact those around me, because it eventually does.

Sound rough? You may not be stoned for partaking in the things the Lord bans, but it will destroy you. Porn will stone you and your reputation. Gossip will stone your character and leave you alone with no allies. Jealousy will stone your future and steal from what could be because you are obsessed with what others have. Unforgiveness stones your mind and hardens your heart. An emotional affair stones your intimacy with your spouse and sets you up for a nightmare.

We must keep ourselves from the things the Lord bans. Our private lives should mirror who we are publicly or the double life will eventually catch up with us. Make a clean start today. Are you who you say you are? Do you do what you say you are going to do? As we close, consider if there are areas in your life lacking in integrity. This may be a good time to confess some of the areas you know are not right. Take some time to ask God to forgive you and move forward into a life of integrity. It's as simple as a decision. And a reminder, this chapter convicted me first, sweet reader! I adore you! Let's get stronger with our integrity together.

Chapter Twelve

I AM A CONQUEROR

My eyes glazed over the homework assignment. We were participating in a marriage class, and I was annoyed. I didn't need homework. We had enough to do. Eddie and I were several years into our marriage and at this point had only Grace and Jude. They were still young, and as any moms of toddlers know, marriage homework is the last thing you have time for at this life stage. However, Eddie and I needed it. Some issues had arisen in our marriage and demanded our focus; they needed to be sorted out. We were having a hard time seeing eye to eye, and I knew there would be great benefit in finishing this class. The process of doing so was frustrating to say the least, though.

After we completed the homework, Eddie and I were supposed to watch a video together and then talk about it. This was one more thing I didn't have time for. The class met the next day, so there was no getting around it if we wanted to participate. I actually really liked the lecturer in the video, so that helped. He was an older man who knew his stuff but was also really funny. Hard truths are easy to take when there is a little humor behind them. (Insert winking face emoji.) I have always loved to learn wisdom from older people. I absolutely love just sitting and watching people from generations older than I am converse. I want to know what they know and learn from their wisdom. The teacher in the video would always say things that stuck with me. The video started playing, and I simultaneously watched while folding the never-ending laundry, half focused.

All of a sudden, somewhere between my terrible attitude and the lull in laundry, I was hit hard with a word—*triggers*. The Bible scholar in the video spoke about how things can take you to a place of pain without warning. He explained how triggers could be places, things, smells, or even songs. Triggers can spark something positive, but he was talking specifically about the ones that cause a heightened sense of pain or fear. He spoke candidly about his own life and how, for his spiritual health and the health of his marriage, he identified his triggers and where they came from. He used the Bible to dispose the power they held over him.

I could feel my heart pounding as he spoke. I tried to hold back tears. The video teaching was suddenly extremely important to me. I sat down, turned up the volume, and listened to the scholar speak about this life-giving principle. It felt so freeing. Eddie noticed my body language was completely different at this point. When the video concluded, we had one of the most profound conversations in our marriage to date.

● ● ●

This word *trigger* gave a verbal definition to what I felt at times but could not articulate. Eddie would do incredibly innocent things that I would react to in terror, insecurity, and fear. It was a battle we tried to master for years, but we failed in achieving a total breakthrough.

One example of a trigger for me was surprises. I hated them and still do. When Eddie would do things to surprise me, they always seemed to end in a fight or put me in a place of fear. I didn't have any idea why until I listened to the video. I realized I'd associated a surprise with a bad thing ever since my first marriage. When you come from a history of domestic violence, especially if the abuse came from a previous spouse, you learn abuse is always something sudden. It takes you by surprise and it's terrifying. Therefore, for years I always hated surprises, not realizing it was because I associated them with the horror of abuse.

On our one-year wedding anniversary, Eddie walked into the house and told me to pack my things because he was taking me on a surprise getaway. Immediately I felt defensive but had no idea why. Being five months pregnant, I scrambled to pack for the weekend. My head was completely spinning with anxiety as to what to bring. Eddie would not tell me where we were going or what we were going to do, and I could feel myself getting angry. We traveled to a bed-and-breakfast, which I had never stayed at before, and I had no idea we had to share a bathroom with strangers as well as eat with them for breakfast. Needless to say, the weekend of our first anniversary was a complete fail. On the way home, we didn't speak much. I knew that Eddie had tried to do something nice, but I couldn't articulate why it seemed so offensive until we sought counseling.

The teaching began to change my perspective, but I knew it was only the beginning. I wanted the exact marriage God desired for me to have, but I realized there were mentalities I needed to unlearn or conquer. I had to dispossess places in my mind in order to possess an incredible marriage filled with freedom and not bondage.

BIG PICTURE

When looking at the Rahab story as a whole, we don't do it justice unless we step back and survey the bigger story God unfolded through the nation of Israel. Jericho was part of a much greater plan and rooted in a promise God gave Abraham long before Rahab was on the scene. In Genesis 12:1–3, God says to Abraham, "Go forth from your country, and from your relatives and from your father's house, to the land which I will show you; and I will make you a great nation, and I will bless you, and make your name great; and so you shall be a blessing; and I will bless those who bless you, and the one who curses you I will curse. And in you all the families of the earth will be blessed."

These words were the beginning of something extraordinary and supernatural. God told Abraham he would make out of him a great nation, give him land, and bless him. These promises were guaranteed by a covenant God made with Abraham officially in Genesis 15:1–21.

Even though they were older, Abraham and Sarah finally had a son, whom they named Isaac. The miraculous birth of Isaac set God's plans further into motion. Hang with me here through a few of the pivotal historical events! I'm going to geek out on you again, but it sets the background for what follows and gets good! Like, so good.

From Isaac was born Jacob, and through Jacob came the heads of the twelve tribes of the nation of Israel. They settled in Egypt because of a great famine, but Joseph, one of the twelve, had been elevated to a position of power and influence by the hand of God prior to this season. He protected and provided for his extended family during this time of lacking. As time passed, the Israelites multiplied and grew tremendously.

By the time God met Moses at the burning bush, Israel wasn't a small group of brothers anymore, but a large group of people working as slaves for the Egyptian people. God worked through Moses to release the Israelites from their life of slavery and lead them through the desert to the land of Canaan. It's about to get so good!

Remember, according to God's promise to Abraham, his descendants would be given "all the land of Canaan" (Genesis 17:8). This land was their inheritance, purposed by God and part of his covenant with them. Numbers 34:13–15 breaks down what piece of land was given to each tribe. Guess what was at the entrance to the heartland of Canaan? Jericho. Yep. The city of Jericho was the first land Israel was purposed to conquer. Now enter our girl Rahab. Okay, here we go.

DO THE WORK OF DISPOSSESSION

Rahab's piece of the story in Jericho was a pivotal piece in what God had been doing for years. In order for Israel to take up residence in the land of Canaan, God commanded them to dispossess the nations already settled there. To dispossess meant they had to defeat the nations that already lived there. They had to put them out of occupancy. For generations and generations, other people groups lived in Canaan. In Numbers 33:51–53, the Lord spoke to Moses, who was leading the people at that time, and said, "Speak to the people of Israel and say to them, When you pass over the Jordan into the land of Canaan, then you shall drive out all the inhabitants of the land from before you and destroy all their figured stones and destroy all their metal images and demolish all their high places. And you shall take possession of the land and settle in it, for I have given the land to you to possess it" (ESV).

Let me break this down because this gets me excited. God told Moses that Israel would have to defeat the people who were already in the promised land before they could take possession of it. God continues in Numbers 33:55 with a warning: "But if you do not drive out the inhabitants of the land from before you, then it shall come about that those whom you let remain of them will become as pricks in your eyes and as thorns in your sides, and they will trouble you in the land in which you live."

God's warning to Israel was clear. His warning was not an attack on innocent people but judgment against their abominable sins. In the case of Jericho, *everything* would have to go. God clearly says to Moses that if the Israelites disobeyed, the enemy would become "pricks in your eyes and as thorns in your sides." Have you ever gotten something in your eye? It's horrible—especially if you wear contact lenses!

One time last year I woke up in the middle of the night with an extremely itchy eye. I woke Eddie and told him to check my eye. He, being very laid-back, said it was fine. The next morning it was full of puss, swollen, itchy, and painful. I know. So gross. I freaked out and went to the eye doctor for her to tell me I had pink eye. Not kidding. I thought I was going to die. I definitely needed to get that thing taken care of ASAP! I thought about the pain of my eye when reading this passage in Numbers. No one wants to live with pink eye day in and day out, yet how many of us are internally living with that kind of irritation because we haven't fought and done the work to dispossess a Jericho from our life?

I find this very powerful truth isn't really talked about much. We all want to invade and possess our promised land, high-fiving one another in our lands of milk and honey, but we don't want to do the work of dispossessing. There are things in our lives to be conquered before we can inhabit our Canaan. In Exodus 23:31–33, God summarizes why we must first dispossess in order to truly conquer: "I will deliver the inhabitants of the land into your hand, and you will drive them out before you. . . . They shall not live in your land, because they will make you sin against Me; for if you serve their gods, it will surely be a snare to you." We cannot live fully and powerfully in our promised lands coexisting with things God has declared that we need to get rid of. Israel and Jericho were never meant to be neighbors.

They would have warred constantly, and the Canaanites' presence would have been a "prick," "thorn," and Israel's downfall, making the Israelites "sin against" God.

— • • • —

Dispossessing a certain mentality or an addiction takes an incredible amount of work. But if we don't conquer the bad first, the full impact of the good is tainted, if not lost. Any bit of the enemy residing in our Jerichos will be pricks and thorns. The enemy will cause discomfort, distraction, blindness, and hurt. Who wants to live in that?

There are Jerichos that need to be conquered in you. Maybe you can resonate with my story above about my and Eddie's marriage. You know and believe your marriage is fully ordained by God to be beautiful, but you've not done the work yet. Your relationship is suffering because of unhealthy mind-sets you developed prior to marriage. Guys, I see this all the time. Women and men live with hurt for thirty-plus years, never dealing with hate, unforgiveness, and bitterness. They've not dispossessed a Jericho from their lives, so they don't experience peace in their land of promise. It's not going to happen unless you dispossess.

Pornography is a major Jericho that men and women—whether married or not—need to conquer. Porn is poison, and it's not just a guy's problem. How can you fully enjoy your mate when you are messing with this destructive Jericho in your marriage? It must be dispossessed.

How about your parenting? When God gives us children, there is a clear mandate to train them in the way they should go, not friend them all the way there. Kids need to be trained and taught how to respect, obey, and so forth. Many parents are doing great jobs, but we all know of someone who parents out of major insecurity rather than authority. He or she has brought a Jericho of insecurity into the promised land of parenthood. The children end up far too often with a "friend" to boss around rather than a parent who will lovingly train them. How about the single person? When God brings the one he has for you into your life, will you grade him or her by past failed relationships and feelings of rejection you have encountered? Are you open to everyone, or do you typecast people because you have dated someone like them in your past? Could it be that without dispossessing the Jericho of rejection you may not fully enjoy the relationship that God brings into your life?

Dispossessing a Jericho will take work, and it must be done with the Lord's help. Israel didn't march around Jericho without the Lord's guidance or power. The Israelites did it with him. They literally took the steps necessary to defeat the enemy. Your steps to dispossessing your Jericho may involve counseling, accountability, or time in the Word. Maybe you need to seek forgiveness, extend forgiveness, or even fast. What steps will lead you to victory? Your obedience brings you closer to dispossessing the things not meant to be there. Drive out the inhabitants to get rid of the thorns and pricks. Or they will bother you the rest of your life. I adore you, sweet reader, but let's to the work.

POSSESSING

Instead of dispossessing a Jericho, what if you don't enter the promised land at all because of the Jericho? Allow me to switch gears here. When some people look at what God has deemed as their promised land, they don't believe it is theirs because someone or something else resides there. The residence of something else intimidates them. Maybe they don't take God at his Word. Or maybe they devalue themselves too much to go for it. The promised land scares them, frustrates them, or makes them angry. Intimidation cripples them and they don't go after the possession at all.

Can you imagine if Moses or Joshua didn't lead the Israelites toward the promised land because people lived there already? What if the two spies saw the fortified city of Jericho and the strength of its people and turned back to camp? Can you hear the defeated report they could have brought back to Joshua? "So, Joshua, someone lives there already. Maybe God has another place in mind for us." The Israelites had to believe in their rightful inheritance in the first place in order to possess it.

It's the same for us. If you are a child of God, you have an inheritance with your name on it. Let me explain. If you're single, maybe there's a man or woman you're interested in, but he or she currently has a girlfriend or boyfriend. Maybe God has even told you that person is who he has for you, but you freak out and don't do anything because he or she seems attached to someone else. Now, I'm not saying to be ridiculous and try to break up the relationship, but I am saying if God has spoken to you about someone and another person is taking up residency in your promised land, wait it out. Pray and ask God to move. If God is truly in it, he will work it out. Don't retreat. Don't avoid. Just let God work.

This also can be true if you are looking for a promotion at your job. Maybe you believe you will move into the boss's position, but your boss hasn't gone anywhere else! Someone else clearly resides in the place God told you is yours. Do not give up. Wait it out. Just like Jericho was leveled with a shout, a boss can be moved or removed in an instant. Don't let the existence of someone else in your promised land threaten your faith in God. He will maneuver you forward when the timing is right.

I remember having a conversation with a pastor not long after revealing I would be starting a women's ministry. He looked at me with frustration on his face and said, "Why do you think we need another women's ministry?" He alluded to the abundance of existing women's ministries and questioned why I would waste my time. I was able to confidently say, "Because God told me to do it." Just because there were other women's ministries out there, I wasn't going to be intimidated out of my promised land. I knew God would make a place for the one he wanted me to start.

Our responsibility is to possess the promise. It's not God's fault if you don't possess your land—it's your fault. Don't blame God for your lack of obedience.

Now in my best cheerleader voice . . . it's time to conquer. Go for it! Possess the promised land, and yield to God's perfect timing and opportunity!

LITTLE BY LITTLE

God will clear a path before you little by little as you conquer the land. My life changed several years ago when I was charging after my very own promised land. I was going ninety miles an hour too fast, against the promise of God to clear the land before me little by little.

Referring to the conquest of Canaan, Deuteronomy 7:22 says, "The LORD your God will clear away these nations before you little by little; you will not be able to put an end to them quickly, for the wild beasts would grow too numerous for you." This concept changed this blonde-haired, lipstick-wearing girl's ambitious heart. God was going to do it, but it was going to be done little by little, "until [I] have increased and possess the land" (Exodus 23:30 ESV).

Because God loved Israel, he cleared the nations before the

Israelites little by little. He didn't do it all at once. After they defeated and dispossessed Jericho, they moved on to Ai, the next city.

There is something about the little-by-little concept I kind of hate, even though I mostly love it. Little by little grates against the all-at-once mentality of go-getters like myself. It stands in contrast to going "viral," "getting rich quick," or "love at first sight." It slows us down to God's reality. He is certainly more than able to bring about miraculous results in an instant—and he does! But most often he fulfills his promises little by little in a way that's best for us.

This pace keeps us centered when we watch someone else's social media and get jealous. They're married with a baby two seconds later and then they buy a house. You know how hard it is to watch accelerated goodness hit others upside the head when you're still waiting for yours? God gives you the promised land little by little.

God's reasoning behind the concept is powerful. Think through the implications of what would have happened if all the land was cleared for the Israelites at once. Not to gross you out, but after the defeat and dispossession of Jericho, there were dead people everywhere. This likely attracted wild beasts. The inhabitants of Jericho had to defend and protect themselves from the literal wild beasts around their city when they lived there. If God had decided to clear the promised land all at the same time, there would have been no one there to protect against the wild beasts. God chose to do it little by little as a way of physically protecting Israel.

Think about it. Possessing too much too soon will create beasts you don't even know about. For instance, it seems everyone wants to be famous. But how many overnight sensations end up doing crazy stuff with their lives? They possessed too much too soon, and the wild beasts of lust, relational strife, or immaturity ran them over. Most likely they didn't realize the danger of having so much fame.

Can you imagine the "beasts" of friends and acquaintances who suddenly wanted to be close to them simply to earn their fifteen minutes of fame?

Exodus 23:30 says, "Little by little I will drive them out from before you, until you have increased and possess the land" (ESV). Just as we are protected from an overload of wild beasts, maybe, too, God wants us to undergo a gradual process until we "have increased." Maybe you're just not ready for portions of your promised land. Just maybe we need to increase in maturity, experiences, training, humility, discipline, and more. This is still the goodness and protection of God at work in our lives.

———— •••• ————

As you read through this chapter, what areas in your life did God point out that need to be dispossessed before you can experience everything he has for you? Understand it is a loving God who gives us what he promised in *his* ways. Oftentimes this is done little by little for our best interest. God wants our hearts undivided for him in our promised lands, rid of the distractions of thorns and pricks. Then we can conquer what we are given.

Chapter Thirteen

I AM NEW

On May 11, 2004, I stood arm in arm with Eddie Miles. The only sounds were the songs of the birds and the wind as it caught the trees. The leaves danced as if to celebrate their attendance at our wedding.

We opted for an outside wedding in a small town outside of Lynchburg, Virginia. After Eddie proposed in November, we were sure we wanted to be married fast. No long engagement needed for us. We were in love and couldn't wait to be husband and wife. The previous six months had been a blur of excitement. Eddie, not being your typical groom, joined me at every wedding appointment. He didn't want to miss out on anything, and I was starting to depend on someone for the first time in a long time (other than the Lord, that is). For so long I had been severely independent in an unhealthy way. I didn't trust anyone, but Eddie was someone God gave me to share life with; not to replace him, but to be my partner for my future.

He was a safe place for me. Eddie wholeheartedly supported and encouraged every dream God gave me. If I am being 100 percent honest, it took me a while to believe him when he spoke things like:

"I support you," "I want you to do everything God told you," "One day I will sell product at your product table," and "I see the call of God on your life." After a while I realized he did believe everything he said, and my heart slowly learned to trust again. I didn't hesitate when he asked me to spend the rest of my life with him. And here we were.

The ambiance of that moment during our ceremony is cemented in my mind. I wore a mermaid, strapless cream dress with sheer ruffles all the way down. Tiny crystal flowers adorned each ruffle. My hair was a masterpiece, swept up with and held in by a crown upside down in the back (which I thought was amazing). Tulle and flowers were woven into it. Eddie stood beside me boasting a black tuxedo with a chocolate-brown vest and a blush-rose corsage. Both of us were crying.

This wasn't just a wedding. It was a new beginning for me. It represented a miracle of God's grace and power. It was a public moment of a promise regarding redemption God made to me in private. He had set me free from so much, and now he was giving me a new start and a second chance.

After the divorce from my first husband, I resolved never to marry again. I wasn't looking for it. Honestly, after what I endured, I preferred remaining single for the rest of my life rather than going through a bad marriage again. It had cost me too much. No marriage was worth the bondage of abuse. So I told God, "It's okay, I only want to marry if it's what you have for me." But God is not amused by our settlements in his name. He wants us to experience abundance. I sensed a rebuttal from him: "No, I am going to do something great with the pain you have surrendered to me." Shortly after, Eddie Miles entered my life.

The songs of the birds grew quiet for just a moment as the officiate in the wedding asked, "Who gives this woman to be married to this man?" My dad stepped forward wearing a gray suit with a blush corsage. He paused to gain the strength to speak. He was emotional yet strong. His answer is one of the things I remember most about our wedding ceremony. He did not give the simple, expected response. He instead proceeded with a beautiful monologue of what our family had encountered in the past and the joy of this moment. He spoke of God's goodness and the responsibility Eddie had to partner with God. He spoke of second chances and the grace of God.

Not an eye was dry as my dad finished. So many were well aware of the cost he had endured because of my previous abusive marriage. Because of his support of me throughout my divorce, he was fired from his church, deemed an outcast, and lost many relationships.

He ended his beautiful response with the father's typical answer, "Her mother and I do," and we entered into the remainder of our ceremony. Old things were gone and new things had come. I was possessing a promised land that God designed for me.

A NEW LINE FOR RAHAB

I've thought so very long and hard about our girl Rahab the harlot. I dare say the end of her life inspires me more than the beginning. After the walls fell down flat on the seventh day of Israel's march, Rahab was rescued. On the next day, day eight, she began a completely new life. On the eighth day she was no longer known as a harlot; she immediately took up the title *hero*. Odds are the nation of Israel didn't even know she was a harlot. All the Israelites knew was that a woman had helped the spies, which had led to their freedom. New title. New way of life. New people. She walked into the new on the eighth day.

The number eight in the Bible symbolizes new beginnings, a new era, and a new season.[24] Rahab fully epitomized this as she walked into what was in store for her on the other side of Jericho's rubble.

Not only did Israel possess the promised land, she began to possess it in her own life as well.

In Matthew 1:5, we discover that she married a man by the name of Salmon. Some scholars believe Salmon was one of the two spies she hid on her roof in the flax. Although it is debated since the spies' names aren't specifically mentioned, we do know Salmon's father was Nahshon. According to Numbers 1, Nahshon was the leader of the tribe of Judah during their early wilderness wanderings, so it seems likely his son would have taken his place upon his death. Continuing in the genealogy of Matthew 1, Salmon and Rahab bore a son by the name of Boaz. We learn that Boaz was the father of Obed by Ruth, Obed was the father of Jesse, and Jesse was the father of King David. This is the bloodline of Jesus!

If you consider the bloodline of Jesus, the story of Rahab should encourage you to the core. Let me break it down even more. The honorable Boaz married Ruth. Ruth's journey is a beautiful story of redemption, but I am also inclined to believe it's an even greater story of redemption for Rahab. Think about it.

Rahab the harlot, the woman who engaged in sex with different men in exchange for money, aligned herself with God. Her life was radically changed as a result. She forsook the false gods of her people and partnered with God in his amazing plan to defeat Jericho. She got a total do-over and transitioned into a new life among the people of God. She married an Israelite and was blessed with the gift of a child—Boaz.

Boaz is revered highly in the Bible as an upright and righteous man. He lived up to his character when he redeemed the foreign and poor widow Ruth. He extended love and a second chance to her in a beautiful way. Even today, Boaz gets so much respect among women. You'll hear some women throw around the phrase "I am looking for my Boaz." But I think maybe we are overlooking where he learned the grace of the second chance.

Don't you think Boaz must have learned the value of the second chance from the strong and powerful influence of his mother, Rahab the harlot, and his father, Salmon? If anyone knew about the power of grace, it was Rahab. If anyone knew about the power of redemption, it was Rahab. If anyone could have appreciated a new beginning when all seemed lost, it was Rahab. No doubt she drilled the theology of grace into her son's sweet head. Deuteronomy 6:7 says, "You shall teach [the commandments of God] diligently to your sons and shall talk of them when you sit in your house and when you walk by the way and when you lie down and when you rise up." Boaz may get too much credit as the man who gave a woman a second chance, because it's clear to me he learned to do so from his mom.

Boaz, a man of position, strength, and wealth, respectfully decided to marry Ruth, a woman with nothing who needed a chance at redemption. God's way is incredible. This bold move can do so much for our own hope.

* * *

Let's step back once more for a bird's-eye view of the genealogy of Jesus. We know Rahab the harlot was the great-great-grandmother of King David. As a woman chosen by God, she was placed in one of the highest forms of honor any woman could receive to be in the direct bloodline of Jesus. Her decision to align herself with God set in motion a life of ministry extending far beyond her initial help to the Israelites. It changed her life, but it impacted generations to come. It is interesting to me that when we see Jesus in the Gospels, he is reaching out to those who needed a second chance. He went to the well to meet the woman who had had five husbands and told her that what she really needed was his living water. He stood with the woman caught in adultery while the Pharisees were ready to stone her and offered grace and forgave her. He was delighted to go and dine with Zacchaeus the tax collector, a villain in biblical times. Jesus was always quick to offer grace. Could it be that Rahab, one of his great-grandmothers, helped to influence how he responded to women and valued them all throughout his days ministering? It was very clear that Jesus valued women no matter their background, and I cannot help but believe that the great compassion he gave them was not only the heart of God the Father but a nod to his heritage.

God ushered in new for Rahab in ways only he could. And as much as we can surmise, she grabbed hold of it. Let's look at the latter part of her life for a few principles we can practice in our new too.

Possess Everything He Has for You

Joshua 1:3 says, "Every place on which the sole of your foot treads, I have given it to you, just as I spoke to Moses." What God promised Israel was there for the taking by his sovereignty, but it did not negate Israel's responsibility to possess it. Rahab was given a new life, a new people, a new faith, a husband, and a new future because she chose to forsake the old. In the last chapter, we talked about dispossessing the land, but in the same breath we must choose to possess. Rahab married Salmon and possessed a life far exceeding the restrictive walls of Jericho. She chose the new and clearly did new well. She, together with her husband, raised Boaz with a healthy fear, respect, and knowledge of the Lord.

What do you need to possess? What do you need to walk into no matter the fear or insecurity you may be feeling? Is your past or the way you view your past preventing you from walking boldly forward into your promised land? Are you struggling to accept the new God has already established for you? Do you feel guilty about living new because of what you did in Jericho? Dispossess the things that hinder and start walking in the new life. Jericho is gone! Move forward.

Don't Rebuild Jericho When You Were Made to Defeat Ai

I find it awesome that there was no chance for Rahab to go back to Jericho. The city was demolished and everyone was dead. Not to mention, the Israelites also burned it. Nothing compelling remained there for her. Sometimes, though, the Jericho life seems easier. What is familiar to us creates a sense of comfort, even if it's truly not the best for us. If we are not careful, we can find ourselves back along the streets of our Jericho with a desire to rebuild it. Do not go back. You have to be a gangster about your decision.

Listen to what Joshua says about Jericho in Joshua 6:26: "Then Joshua made them take an oath at that time, saying, 'Cursed before the LORD is the man who rises up and builds this city Jericho; with the loss of his firstborn he shall lay its foundation, and with the loss of his youngest son he shall set up its gates.'" Those are some hardcore words for Israel. No doubt Rahab was listening loud and clear. It was the first recorded thing she heard Joshua say after being rescued, and it was bold. "Do not rebuild Jericho or it will cost you!" I'm sure those words rang in her ears until the moment of her death.

Interestingly enough a man by the name of Hiel of Bethel decided to rebuild Jericho. First Kings 16:34 says, "In Ahab's time, Hiel of Bethel rebuilt Jericho. He laid its foundations at the cost of his firstborn son Abiram, and he set up its gates at the cost of his youngest son Segub, in accordance with the word of the LORD spoken by Joshua son of Nun" (NIV). I shivered as I read this. Hiel decided to defy the Word of the Lord and rebuilt something that God clearly did not want rebuilt. And just as Joshua said, it came to pass.

Jericho can call to us and bid us to rebuild, but if we do so, it will cost us more than we are willing to pay. Proverbs 26:11 says, "Like a dog that returns to its vomit is a fool who repeats his folly." Do not return to your former sinful ways. It will only be worse. I challenge you here and now to rebuke anything in your life that would lead you to rebuild what God has freed you from. The temptation may entice, the habit may whisper to you, or the thought pattern may scream, but you will pay severely if you rebuild what God has torn down.

You were made to move forward. My life was changed when I decided to walk in the new and keep feelings of inadequacy, shame, and guilt in my past. I had to move on from being the "divorcée" and accept I was walking as a new person. No one can choose to walk in the new for you but you. You have to change you own life. The next piece of the promised land awaits, and you are promised victory. Forget Jericho and step up to the plate of defeating Ai.

Woman, Walk in the Leadership the Lord Appoints to You

Don't worry. I am not going to go off on a girl-power rant. Although I do love me some girl power. (Insert fire emoji.) I believe you cannot divorce Rahab's identity as a woman from her favorable position, leadership, and heroic faith. God could have chosen a man to hide the spies in the flax. He could have chosen a man to be heralded as the hero of this story, but in his wisdom, sovereignty, and favor, he chose a woman. A strong woman who led men to safety because of her counsel and courage. The spies listened to her as a woman and her guidance saved a nation, which is what God planned.

If I had a nickel for every time someone told me God doesn't want me in a position of leadership in ministry because I am a woman, it would be an embarrassing audit on the state of the church. We have deleted countless messages from my social media when the messages shame me from sharing about Jesus because I am woman. It's disgraceful. The Great Commission wasn't made just for men, but also for women. It is there for me. Women have been chided and disrespected for centuries, even when God clearly appoints them to an area of leadership and ministry. Are we silencing Rahabs, Esthers, Marys, and the like because we are so caught up in making sure we don't let women have too much of a voice? We must unlearn legalism in this area and affirm the women God has asked to serve for his name.

There is no denying Rahab's direct effect on all of our lives, not just those of women. She wasn't just a women's minister; her sacrificial ministry has led us all. She led because she was called. Woman, as you are reading this and find your heart beating out of your chest because God has called you to an area of leadership or ministry, go forward and possess the land. Draw your strength from the pages of God's Word and the approval of his appointment. Don't be discouraged when faced with opposition, but rather humbly defer to the Lord. Every time I am chided with a legalistic mind-set of rejection for being a woman in ministry, I point my opposer to the God who appointed me. After all, man's criticism doesn't erase God's assignment.

Your Past Will Not Be a Hindrance to You

I thought for a second my past would hinder me from ministry or my promised land of marriage and kids, but the craziest thing happened. It actually proved to be my biggest asset. When God redeems us, he supernaturally changes things we thought would harm or disqualify us and instead makes them into something good. Philippians 3:13–14 says, "I do not regard myself as having laid hold of it yet; but one thing I do: forgetting what lies behind and reaching forward to what lies ahead, I press on toward the goal for the prize of the upward call of God in Christ Jesus."

I can honestly say I am so thankful for the pain and the hardship because it has propelled me into a life of purpose. If your past is full of pain, God is your Healer. If your past is full of sin, confess your sins, for "He is faithful and righteous to forgive us our sins and to cleanse us from all unrighteousness" (1 John 1:9). If your past is full of shame, none of those who put their hope in him will be ashamed. If your past is full of confusion, he is the God of peace. Our pasts don't go away, but they don't have to be a hindrance to us either. God makes all things new.

NOW GO LIVE IN THE NEW!

Now, you have to act, just as Rahab acted. This is YOUR LIFE! This is your moment! Find yourself in Rahab and apply the principles in your life. You have the opportunity to be the hero you want to be. Push beyond the past and embrace what God is calling you out of. You were written into his story, and he wants to see all you can become!

Behold, I have made you a new, sharp threshing sledge with double edges; you will thresh the mountains and pulverize them, and will make the hills like chaff. (Isaiah 41:15)

Behold, I will do something new, now it will spring forth; will you not be aware of it? I will even make a roadway in the wilderness, rivers in the desert. (Isaiah 43:19)

And He who sits on the throne said, "Behold, I am making all things new." And He said, "Write, for these words are faithful and true." (Revelation 21:5)

[O]ur old self was crucified with Him, in order that our body of sin might be done away with, so that we would no longer be slaves to sin. (Romans 6:6)

[P]ut on the new self, which in the likeness of God has been created in righteousness and holiness of the truth. (Ephesians 4:24)

DISCUSSION QUESTIONS

Chapter One
I AM RAHAB

• • •

1. There are times in our lives when it is helpful to share things we've kept hidden. James 5:16 says, "Therefore confess your sins to each other and pray for each other so that you may be healed" (NIV). Consider if there is an area you should share with a trusted loved one. Before you speak with him or her, be sure you have been honest before the Lord first, confessing your sin and receiving his forgiveness.

2. Even though initially it may be hard to relate to the lives of Mary or Esther, their lives are still a reflection of the power of God and his truth. Read Luke 1:26–56 or Esther 1–8. What circumstances or things worked against these two women, and who was God in the midst of them?

3. Do you believe you are a part of a bigger story? God's story? Why or why not? His story will be greater than you can dream. Pray this: *Lord, I want your dream for me.*

4. Read Psalm 139:23–24 as a prayer: "Search me, God, and know my heart; test me and know my anxious thoughts. See if there is any offensive way in me, and lead me in the way everlasting" (NIV). Is there public or private sin in your life with too much power over you? How has it defined you?

5. Write down your own definition of the figurative meaning of harlot.

6. Gratitude for what Jesus accomplished on the cross helps us shift from focusing on our sin to focusing on the greatness of Christ. Choose one of the following verses and commit it to memory this week.
   - "But thanks be to God! He gives us the victory through our Lord Jesus Christ!" (1 Corinthians 15:57 NIV)
   - "'He himself bore our sins' in his body on the cross, so that we might die to sins and live for righteousness; 'by his wounds you have been healed.'" (1 Peter 2:24 NIV)

- "If our hearts condemn us, we know that God is greater than our hearts, and he knows everything." (1 John 3:20 NIV)

7. Autumn believed she could be a hero for the kingdom of God. Read John 14:12 and describe how this relates to the definition of being a hero. What does it mean to you?

Chapter Two
I AM AUTUMN

——— • • • ———

1. Revelation 12:11 (NIV) says, "They triumphed over him [the enemy] by the blood of the Lamb and by the word of their testimony . . ." In other words, victory continues for believers as they maintain their testimony of trust in who God is and what Jesus accomplished on the cross.

   • How was this idea of triumph exemplified when Autumn began sharing her personal story with others?

   • Write down your testimony if you haven't before. Share a portion of your story God has come in and altered.

2. Autumn was anxious about what her divorce title would keep her from in the future. Are there things you fear may be withheld or ruined about your future because of former or current sins? What are those things? What does God's Word say about our future according to Jeremiah 29:11?

3. Reflect on your negative or positive titles and how they impact you.

- List some of the ways others define you. These are your publicly assigned labels.

- Now list some of the ways you have titled yourself. These are your self-given titles.

4. Understanding and receiving who we are as a God's child is crucial to removing our false titles. Further examples of our identity in Christ can be found in the verses below. Write down what they mean to you.
   - Galatians 2:20

   - 2 Corinthians 5:17

   - John 1:12

   - 2 Corinthians 6:18

5. In your own words, what does it mean for you to be God's child? Review the descriptions in the chapter as needed.

6. Incorrect titles are removed by identifying them, confessing them, and then replacing them with the ones we have as children of God. Use the prayer below as a guide and allow the truth of God's Word to speak to your true title.

> *Father, search my heart and reveal any of the false titles in my life, even the good ones I have allowed to be more important than what you say about me. Forgive me for operating as anything less than who I am in you. Forgive me for my own destructive self-talk.*
>
> *You say I am a child of God, so I come into agreement now with this. I am chosen. I am righteous. I am seen. I am fearless. I am purposed for greatness in your astounding story. I am made for relationship with you. I belong. I have everything I need for living life fully. I am free.*
>
> *Thank you for the sacrifice of your Son, Jesus, on the cross, whose death conquered the power of sin once and for all. I give sin no more authority in my life but submit to the powerful resurrection authority living in me through your Spirit, which is greater.*
>
> *Thank you, Jesus. Amen.*

Chapter Three
I AM NOT ONE SEASON

— • • • —

1. Rahab did not know the significance of drying flax on her roof during harvest season, but it served as the context for rescue and abundance in her life. Can you relate? Has there been something seemingly mundane or even demanding of your time and effort that God used to propel you further?

2. The natural seasons are composed of the following: soil preparation, sowing, growth, pruning, harvest, and utilization of the harvest. What season of life do you feel like you are in primarily right now? Why?

3. The season of root development is pivotal. We are to root ourselves in Jesus in order to face life's trials and bear fruit. How are you doing this?

4. Consider the promise of Psalm 126:5–6: "Those who sow in tears shall reap with joyful shouting. He who goes to and fro weeping, carrying his bag of seed, shall indeed come again with a shout of joy, bringing his sheaves with him." Write down the

areas in which you feel like you are sowing in tears. By faith, thank the Lord in advance for the promise of joyful reaping over those areas. Ask him to help you with any unbelief.

5. Spend some time writing down the seasons of life God has walked you through. Consider how God used each of them to bring you to the next one. How do they show God's faithfulness?

Chapter Four
I AM LISTENING

———— • • • ————

1. The Holy Spirit lives in us as believers and is one of the main ways we hear the voice of God. Read the following verses to further understand the role of the Spirit in our lives.
   - Comforter—John 14:16–17
   - Counselor/Wisdom—John 16:13; Galatians 5:18
   - Intercessor—Romans 8:26
   - Power—John 14:12; Acts 1:8
   - Strengthener—Galatians 5:16–23; Romans 8:12–14

2. What makes it hard for you to listen to the Lord for yourself? Voice those things to God and consider if there are practical things to help. Simple things, like turning off the television earlier each evening or designating a certain space in the house for quiet time with him can be a great starting place.

3. Has there been a Spirit-led no or a closed door in your life? Tell God how you feel about the no and surrender your heart again to his sovereign leading. Hebrews 4:7 says, "Today, if you hear his voice, do not harden your hearts" (NIV). Confess any hardness of heart and allow the Spirit to tend to your disappointment.

4. Share about a time someone has encouraged you with a specific verse or word from the Spirit. Since hearing the voice of the Lord is meant to also change the lives of those around us, spend some time praying for a friend or family member this week. If the timing feels right, maybe you can share what was impressed on your heart for them.

5. Select a Gospel book or a psalm and read it for the next few days. Ask the Holy Spirit to reveal himself to you as you read. Approach it with expectancy. Share what you learned about God in the passage. How did the passage change your heart?

Chapter Five
I AM RISK

———— • • • ————

1. Why is risk an inevitable part of our lives as believers? Why is it riskier to go by what we see?

2. Rahab's risk was fueled, in part, by recounting who God was in the past. Risk-taking for us should also be a time when we keep our eyes on God and recount who he has been in the past. Reflect on instances of God's faithfulness to you when you have stepped out to trust him. What did you learn about God during those moments?

3. What risks are you presently avoiding, if any? What risks are you presently taking in obedience to God? Write down the associated area of fear, intimidation, or discomfort with each risk. Ask God to show you what steps to take next.

4. Journal about a time when you took a risk you believe God called you to, but the result did not turn out as you had hoped. We must remember, obedience to God is up to us, but the results and their timing are in his hands. Pause for a moment and ask the Holy Spirit to show you God's heart for you in the season after the risk. Let him tend to any disappointment, resentment, unhealthy coping mechanism, or mistrust that followed. Memorize Philippians 3:10–11 as a challenging reminder to keep God as your greatest reward, even over the earthly ones.

5. In what ways and to whom are you an "Ambassador for the Lord"? Be specific and write them down. In word and action, we represent Christ and his gospel message. Is there anything you feel like you could do differently in the spheres of influence you've listed?

Chapter Six
I AM FLAWED

• • •

1. Scripture makes it clear Rahab's "white lie" is still a lie. Sin is not minimized or rationalized in the view of our holy God. Read the following verses to see how offenses committed even in our hearts are viewed as a sin to God. How does this impact your view of sin?

    • Matthew 5:27–28: "You have heard that it was said, 'YOU SHALL NOT COMMIT ADULTERY'; but I say to you that everyone who looks at a woman with lust for her has already committed adultery with her in his heart."

    • Exodus 20:17 ESV: "You shall not covet your neighbor's house; you shall not covet your neighbor's wife, or his male servant, or his female servant, or his ox, or his donkey, or anything that is your neighbor's."

2. What sin(s) are you currently struggling with? Confess them before the Lord and receive his forgiveness. Minimize their power in your life by proclaiming Romans 5:1: "Therefore, having been justified by faith, we have peace with God through our Lord Jesus Christ." Commit this verse to memory.

3. Nothing could stop God from being faithful to fulfill his promise to the Israelites, even a flawed Rahab. When was a time you sinned but saw God's faithfulness in spite of it?

4. What is something you believe God is asking you to step out in faith and do, despite your flaws and limitations? What initial step do you need to take?

5. Is there a "Rahab" in your life whom you have judged and excluded, either emotionally or physically, because of their sin? Luke 6:37 says, "Do not judge, and you will not be judged; and do not condemn, and you will not be condemned; pardon, and you will be pardoned." Ask the Lord to forgive you for judging.

Chapter Seven
I AM SACRIFICE

— • • • —

1. Describe a time when you served yourself out of selfishness, but it backfired and left you unfulfilled.

2. In what ways has the selfie world deceived, disillusioned, or discouraged you?

3. Spend some time with the Lord and ask him to show you if there is any area in which you have been serving yourself to an unbalanced degree. Who has been negatively impacted by it? Pray about whether you should talk with anyone or write a letter to ask forgiveness.

4. Proverbs 11:25 says, "The generous man will be prosperous, and he who waters will himself be watered." How can you be generous, maybe even sacrificial, with your time, finances, talents, or gifts this week? Be specific.

5. Galatians 2:20 says, "I have been crucified with Christ; and it is no longer I who live, but Christ lives in me; and the life which I now live in the flesh I live by faith in the Son of God, who loved me and gave Himself up for me." How does the sacrifice of Christ change your perspective about the reasons you sacrifice?

Chapter Eight
I AM GOD'S INSIDE MAN

---•••---

1. Write down the places in which you are physically positioned right now. Include things like your job, your neighborhood, your relationships, and your church. Ask the Lord to help you see your position in those places through his eyes. What do you believe he wants for you in those places?

2. Write down who you are naturally. Include things like your personality, innate talents, or instincts. How has the Lord used these things about you to help you discover more of who he is? How has the Lord used these parts of you in the lives of others? Give thanks to God for those things, as Psalm 139:13–14 encourages: "For You formed my inward parts; You wove me in my mother's womb. I will give thanks to You, for I am fearfully and wonderfully made; wonderful are Your works, and my soul knows it very well."

3. What physical or natural positions in your life make you feel like
    an outsider? Pray Romans 8:28 over those things and commit
    the verse to memory. "And we know that God causes all things
    to work together for good to those who love God, to those who
    are called according to His purpose."

4. God positioned his Son physically among the Jews at a specific
    time in history, but his birth and life were not void of hardship
    and danger. Nor are our appointed places of positioning void of
    trouble or suffering. Read the following verses for encourage-
    ment: John 16:33; Romans 8:35–37.

5. Jesus's own people rejected him. He was viewed as an outsider.
    Yet his position as the Savior of the world remained. Read Isaiah
    53:2–6 and write down the heart-wrenching ways he was viewed
    as an "outsider."

Chapter Nine
I AM A CHANGED WORLD

———•••———

1. How has your faith changed your own personal world? What external behaviors are different? How do you think differently? In what ways do you respond differently from an internal perspective?

2. Read the story of Gideon (Judges 6) or Saul (Acts 9) to see other instances where God first dealt with an individual's heart before his faith extended itself for others.

3. If you are in a season of waiting for the promise, you are still in a season of work. Waiting can feel passive, but there is still either internal or external work to be accomplished. Write down something you're waiting on that you believe God has promised you. What kind of internal discipline or outward work do you believe God is asking you to do in the meantime?

4. How are you stewarding the things God has given you in this season? Include things like how you're stewarding your time, your finances, your resources, and your gifts. Pray about these areas.

5. In Philippians 2:12–13, Paul says, "Just as you have always obeyed, not as in my presence only, but now much more in my absence, work out your salvation with fear and trembling; for it is God who is at work in you, both to will and to work for His good pleasure." We are fully saved when we receive Christ in our lives, but there is a working out to grow in our relationship with him. It is encouraging to know that the desire to do well comes from God at the end of the day. Spend some time praying through this verse and be encouraged to know he partners with you to do the work.

Chapter Ten
I AM ON TIME

———•••———

1. Have you ever made a promise to someone with full intentions of fulfilling it but were delayed before you could? What was the promise, and what delayed you? How did it make you feel?

2. Is there a promise God has called you to believe in him for? Write down the promise and how long ago it was impressed upon your heart. How have you been changed while waiting for the promise to be fulfilled? Read one of the following verses as a reminder of how we are to wait: Psalm 62:5; Psalm 130:5; Isaiah 30:18; Isaiah 64:4.

3. Rahab endured a season of waiting because God was actively working out some things in the Israelites first. Our waiting isn't always directly about us. Can you recall a time you've seen this to be true in your own life?

4. For one of the areas in which you are experiencing a wait right now, what active steps do you believe God wants you to be taking? Are they more spiritual in nature, like spending additional time in prayer and the Word? Or are they more practical steps? List them out and consider how you are doing in them.

Chapter Eleven
I AM INTEGRITY

— • • • —

1. Lamentations 2:17 says, "The LORD has done what He purposed; He has accomplished His word." God is a man of his word. What are some ways you have seen God's integrity and uprightness in your own life?

2. Is there an area in your life where you have said one thing but done another? Or promised one thing but not done it at all? What motivated your decision? Who did it impact? Ask the Lord for forgiveness and consider if there are others in your life you need to ask forgiveness from.

3. What is your view of the Word of God? Do you believe God does what he says he will do? If you are struggling in this, spend some time searching the Scriptures to see where God has maintained his promises. How does this influence you to keep your own word?

4. Write down the ways you describe yourself. Who do you say that you are? Do these align with who God says you are? Are any of these incongruent with who you are in private?

Chapter Twelve
I AM A CONQUEROR

•·•·•

1. Recount how the story of Jericho was a small piece of God's bigger story and covenant with the Israelites.

2. If Israel disobeyed God's commands and didn't dispossess the inhabitants in their promised land, what would their enemy become to them? What effect would it have on the Israelites?

3. Ask the Lord what things in your life need dispossessing. Maybe it's an outward behavior, a tangible item, or something in your heart. We conquer the sin in our lives by replacing it with the truth of God's Word and by depending on his Spirit for the victory.

4. What do you believe is part of your future promised land? Does something or someone else already possess any of those areas? Proverbs 3:5–6 says "Trust in the LORD with all your heart and do not lean on your own understanding. In all your

ways acknowledge Him and He will make your paths straight." Commit this verse to memory and tell the Lord specifically what you trust him for.

5. How has the "little by little" method of victory played out in your life? What benefit has it been to you and others?

Chapter Thirteen
I AM NEW

———•••———

1. Commit these verses to memory (in whatever Bible translation you normally use):
   - Isaiah 41:15
   - Isaiah 43:19
   - Revelation 21:5
   - Romans 6:6
   - Ephesians 4:24

2. Now write out prayers, using these Scriptures in your own words, as a praise to God and a commitment to letting him create something new in your heart.

NOTES

1. Israel P. Loken, *The Old Testament Historical Books: An Introduction* (Xulon Press, 2008), 402.

2. James Strong, "zanah," *The New Strong's Exhaustive Concordance of the Bible*, *Blue Letter Bible*, https://www.blueletterbible.org/lang/lexicon/lexicon.cfm?Strongs=H2181&t=KJV.

3. James Strong, "porne," *The New Strong's Exhaustive Concordance of the Bible*, *Blue Letter Bible*, https://www.blueletterbible.org/lang/lexicon/lexicon.cfm?Strongs=G4204&t=KJV.

4. Flavius Josephus, *Josephus: Antiquities of the Jews*, trans. by William Whitson (Nashville: Thomas Nelson Press, 2003), 80–82.

5. Carolyn Pressler, *Westminster Biblical Companion: Joshua, Judges & Ruth* (Louisville: Westminster John Knox Press, 2002), 24–25.

6. Geoffrey W. Bromiley, *The International Standard Bible Encyclopedia, Volume 4*, ed. Geoffrey W. Bromiley (Grand Rapids, Michigan: Wm. B. Eerdmans Publishing, 1995), 140.

7. Ibid.

8. James Strong, "shama," *The New Strong's Exhaustive Concordance of the Bible*, *Blue Letter Bible*, https://www.blueletterbible.org/lang/lexicon/lexicon.cfm?strongs=H8091.

9. Merriam-Webster, "risk," https://www.merriam-webster.com/dictionary/risk.

10. Crossway Bibles, study note on Hebrews 11:1 in *ESV: Study Bible: English Standard Version* (Wheaton, IL: Crossway Bibles, 2012).

11. James Strong, "justify," *The New Strong's Exhaustive Concordance of the Bible*, *Blue Letter Bible*, https://www.blueletterbible.org/lang/lexicon/lexicon.cfm?Strongs=G1344&t=ESV.

12. Merriam-Webster, "sacrifice," https://www.merriam-webster.com/dictionary/sacrifice.

13. MIT Technology Review, "Data Scientists Chart the Tragic Rise of Selfie Deaths," https://www.technologyreview.com/s/602862/data-scientists-chart-the-tragic-rise-of-selfie-deaths/.

14. Bryant G. Wood, posted May 1, 2008, "The Walls of Jericho," http://www.biblearchaeology.org/post/2008/06/The-Walls-of-Jericho.aspx#Article.

15. Crossway Bibles, study note on Joshua 2:15 in *ESV: Study Bible: English Standard Version* (Wheaton, IL: Crossway Bibles, 2012).

16. Crossway Bibles, *The City of Jericho* in *ESV: Study Bible: English Standard Version* (Wheaton, IL: Crossway Bibles, 2012).

17. Merriam-Webster, "promise," https://www.merriam-webster.com/dictionary/promise.

18. Bible Hub, "Complete Biblical Timeline," http://biblehub.com/timeline/.

19. Mike Holmes, "What Would Happen if the Church Tithed?," *Relevant*, https://relevantmagazine.com/love-and-money/what-would-happen-if-church-tithed.

20. Bible Hub, "Complete Biblical Timeline."

21. http://www.biblearchaeology.org/post/2008/06/The-Walls-of-Jericho.aspx#Article.

22. Merriam-Webster, "integrity," https://www.merriam-webster.com/dictionary/integrity.

23. James Strong, "integrity," *The New Strong's Exhaustive Concordance of the Bible*, *Blue Letter Bible*, https://www.blueletterbible.org/lang/lexicon/lexicon.cfm?Strongs=H8537&t=KJV.

24. E. W. Bullinger, *Number in Scripture: It's Supernatural Design and Spiritual Significance* (Kessinger Publishing, 2003), 200.

ABOUT THE AUTHOR

• • •

AUTUMN MILES is the founder of Autumn Miles Ministries, an organization devoted to spiritually challenging the way women think. She is a dynamic speaker who produces regular inspirational content for her over 80,000 Facebook followers in addition to speaking at conferences nationwide.

As a survivor of domestic abuse, Autumn is passionate about educating the church on how to effectively assist victims. In 2017, Autumn partnered with LifeWay Research to sponsor a study on domestic violence in the church. When the results showed that only 50 percent of churches have a plan in place to respond to domestic violence, she published the pamphlet *10 Steps to Prepare Your Church for Domestic Violence*, which has been used by many churches. She is a passionate advocate for domestic violence victims, women in ministry, and adoption.

Autumn has shared her story of overcoming abuse and finding God's purpose for her life in many media outlets and has made appearances on TLC, *The 700 Club*, Cornerstone TV, and Voice of America. Her writing has appeared on prestigious outlets including the *Washington Post*, Religion News Service, the *Dallas Morning News*, the Blaze, Faithwire, and CafeMom.

Additionally, Autumn is the host of *The Autumn Miles Show*, a daily radio talk show that airs on the Salem Radio Network in Dallas, Texas. On it, she brings her audience bold truth coupled with raw faith. *I Am Rahab* is Autumn's second book. Her first one was *Appointed: Your Future Starts Now*.

Autumn married Eddie Miles in 2004 and has four beautiful children: two biological, Grace and Jude, and two adopted, Moses and Haven. She and her family reside in Dallas, Texas.

For booking information, contact:
gloria@ambassadorspeakers.com

IF YOU ENJOYED THIS BOOK, WILL YOU CONSIDER SHARING THE MESSAGE WITH OTHERS?

Mention the book in a blog post or through Facebook, Twitter, Pinterest, or upload a picture through Instagram.

Recommend this book to those in your small group, book club, workplace, and classes.

Head over to facebook.com/worthypublishing, "LIKE" the page, and post a comment as to what you enjoyed the most.

Post a picture of the book on Instagram with the caption: "I recommend reading #IAmRahab by @autumnmiles // @worthypub"

Pick up a copy for someone you know who would be challenged and encouraged by this message.

Write a book review online.

WORTHY®
PUBLISHING

Visit us at worthypublishing.com

twitter.com/worthypub

instagram.com/worthypub

facebook.com/worthypublishing

youtube.com/worthypublishing